Clothed with Strength and Dignity
Women of the Bible
By Amy Schisler

Amy Schisler

ISBN-13: 979-8-9883677-2-7

Published by:
Chesapeake Sunrise Publishing
Amy Schisler
Bozman, MD
2023

Table of Contents

PREFACE

The women in the Bible have always been intimidating to me because I never knew their stories. I knew their highlight reel rather than the fullness of their truth. "Women of the Bible" presents each woman in the Old and New Testament as real and relatable. I felt as if I could connect with any one of them over a cup of coffee.

As a woman I found myself feeling seen and heard in each digestible narrative. Amy Schisler presents her points with ease to the reader. I never felt intimidated reading her words. For the first time, I felt welcomed by women who have always been there, because Amy made the introductions. As a mother I am grateful to pass the rich legacies of these women on to my daughter. As a daughter of the King, I now appreciate the sisters before me.

These stories are not just for women, they are filled with virtue for every human being. Finally, there is a trove of these treasured stories in one place. Thank you dear sister Amy, you have done a service for us all.

- Liv Harrison, author, speaker, podcaster

"Who can find a woman of worth?
Far beyond jewels is her value."
Proverbs 31:10

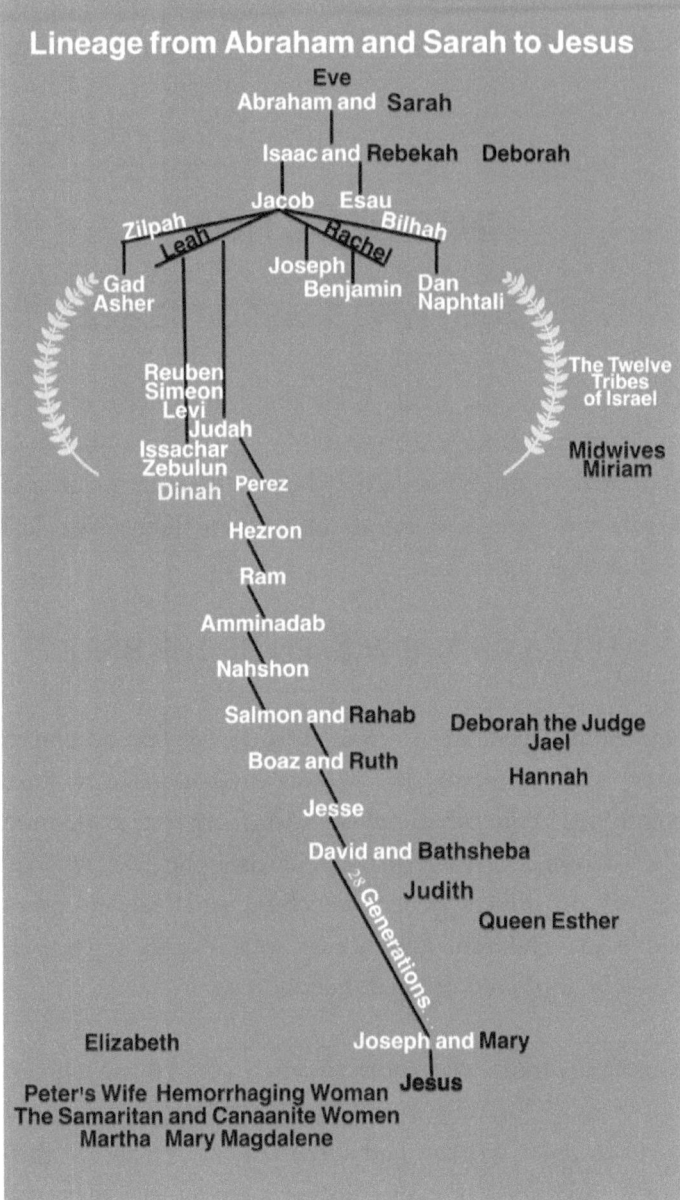

Lineage from Abraham and Sarah to Jesus

Eve
Abraham and Sarah

Isaac and Rebekah   Deborah

Jacob   Esau

Zilpah   Bilhah
Leah   Rachel

Joseph

Gad   Benjamin   Dan
Asher   Naphtali

Reuben   The Twelve
Simeon   Tribes
Levi   of Israel
Judah
Issachar   Midwives
Zebulun   Miriam
Dinah   Perez

Hezron

Ram

Amminadab

Nahshon

Salmon and Rahab   Deborah the Judge
Jael

Boaz and Ruth   Hannah

Jesse

David and Bathsheba

28 Generations   Judith

Queen Esther

Elizabeth   Joseph and Mary

Peter's Wife Hemorrhaging Woman   Jesus
The Samaritan and Canaanite Women
Martha Mary Magdalene

INTRODUCTION

THE WOMEN WHO SHAPED THE BIBLE

The women of the Bible. What does that phrase mean to you? Who were they? What did they do? What do they have to do with Jesus? What do they have to do with me or you? Before we begin looking at the women themselves, let's explore these questions.

WHO WERE THE WOMEN OF THE BIBLE?

Depending upon the source, there are as few as ninety-three and as many as two-hundred-and-five women mentioned in the Bible, and of those, forty-nine are named. These women were wives, mothers, daughters, nursemaids, widows, prostitutes, queens, deceivers, and believers. Some had many children, and others were childless, or were childless until God opened their wombs.

Among the more well-known women, stand those who are but shadows looming in the corners of the Biblical world, yet even those women had some kind of impact on their world and ours. For every mother named Leah, there was a woman who was barren; and for every Mary, there was another woman who spoke for or on behalf of her husband or son. Though the number of men far exceeds the women mentioned in the Bible, often, the women who are mentioned had just as large an impact, and in some cases, a larger impact than their male counterparts.

On my wedding day, my father took the time before he walked me down the aisle, to tell me something I have never forgotten. Instead of saying, be kind to your husband, or be a good mother, or never go to bed angry, or any number of other pieces of advice he could have given me, my father said this, "As a mother, it is up to you to pass along your faith to your children, and as a wife, it is up to you to make sure your husband attends Mass every Sunday and remains faithful to the Church."

I could have heard his words and thought, what a heavy burden to be placed on a twenty-three-year-old just before she makes her wedding vows. Instead, I like to think that, like Mary, I "kept all these things, pondering them in [my] heart" (Luke 2:19). What I have learned over the many years since my father spoke those words to me is that as a *woman*, not just a wife or mother, I am called to bring others to Christ and His Church. I must follow our Blessed Mother's example of humbly participating in God's plan. "God delights in drawing secondary causes into the dense complexity of his providential plan, granting to them the honor of cooperating with him and his designs. The handmaid of the Lord, who is the Mother of the Church, is the humblest of these humble instruments—and therefore the most effective."[1]

As we will see, not just as wives and mothers, but as women from all walks of life, these women have something to teach us. We owe a debt of gratitude to the women of the Bible and to all women who have lived lives of faith. In the words of Saint Pope John Paul the Great, "The Church gives thanks for all the manifestations of the feminine 'genius' which have appeared in the course of history, in the midst of all peoples and nations; she gives thanks for all the charisms which the Holy Spirit distributes to women in the history of the People of God, for all the victories which she owes to their faith, hope, and charity: she gives thanks for all the fruits of feminine holiness."[2]

WHAT DID THE WOMEN OF THE BIBLE DO?

The women shaped the course of their people—Rebekah, Hannah, and the Virgin Mary. They had great influence and power—Deborah, Esther, and Judith. They were the matriarchs of nations—Eve, Sarah, and Ruth.

Many of these women were wives who bore children, tended their homes, and advised their husbands. Sarah and Elizabeth, both advanced in age, bore children to fulfill God's covenants. Though Abraham and Zachariah are exalted as the *Father of Nations* and a man "filled with the Holy Spirit" (Luke 1:67), it was their wives who bore the sons who played mighty roles in the development of both Judaism and Christianity. The Lord told Abraham, "through Isaac shall your descendants be made" (Genesis 21:12). To Zachariah, the angel Gabriel declared,

"Elizabeth will bear you a son...he will be great before the Lord... filled with the Holy Spirit... and he will turn many of the sons of Israel to the Lord their God... to make ready for the Lord a people prepared" (Luke 1:13-17).

Other women bore sons who would advance God's teachings and his mission to bring his peoples to himself. Rebekah bore Jacob; Hannah bore Samuel; Ruth bore Jesse, the father of David; and Mary bore the Messiah. But among the women of the Bible are also warriors such as Deborah and Jael, prophetesses such as Miriam and Anna, and royalty like Bathsheba and Esther. There were women who seemingly did wrong, but who were used by God to fulfill His purposes. Rebekah deceived her husband, the Samaritan woman at the well was an adulteress, and Mary Magdalene was a sinner of untold magnitude. Yet God turned their actions into paths to glory. "Even though you meant harm...God meant it for good, to achieve this present end, the survival of many people" (Genesis 50:20).

No matter their background, status, or holiness, the women of the Bible contributed to the history and advancement of Judaism and Christianity in profound ways. Through them, their children, and their examples, we have some of the greatest teachings of our faith.

WHAT DO THEY HAVE TO DO WITH JESUS?

St. Augustine said, "In the Old Testament the New is concealed, in the New the Old is revealed."[3] Everything that is told in the Old Testament is intrinsically tied to what takes place in the New Testament. The Old Testament tells the story of salvation leading up to the coming of the Messiah which is told in the New Testament. To fully understand the people, occurrences, and covenants fulfilled in the New Testament, we must recognize and understand their development the Old Testament.

Throughout the Old Testament, story after story, person after person, and event after event, we are taken on a journey. This is a journey of time and place, war and peace, good and bad, plenty and scarcity, but the journey has one purpose—to bring God's people back to him. From the fall of Adam and Eve until the birth of Christ, humanity awaited the reunion of God and Man. It is through the women of the Bible, and one young woman in particular in the New Testament, that this reunion is able to take place. The path to the reunification of human beings with God follows the paths of the offspring of Eve through the offspring of Mary.

In this book, we will look at how each of the women who are highlighted played a role in the coming of the Savior or in the furtherance of his mission. This mission continues to be our mission today.

WHAT DO THEY HAVE TO DO WITH ME?

All who are baptized are called to be missionaries, to be priests and prophets, to continue the work of Abraham and

Isaiah and Peter and Paul. We are the modern-day Hannahs who dedicate our children to the Lord. We are the contemporary Ruths who pledge to follow the God of Abraham. We are the new Marys who say yes to God when he calls us. We are the present-day Samaritan Women who tell all within hearing that we have encountered the Christ. We are the twenty-first century Mary Magdalenes who spread the Good News.

Have you ever heard of a cairn? If you're a hiker, you've surely come across them. Traditionally built with stones, but sometimes with sticks, cairns are markers used to represent something and to leave messages to others who pass by. From the Gaelic term càrn, meaning piles of stones, cairns have been used since prehistoric times to

Cairn on Mount Precipice, Nazareth

designate a place of meaning—burial monuments, ceremonial purposes, buried treasure or caches of food, or to mark trails. Cairns have been discovered dating back as far as around 2400 B.C.

As you read this book and do the accompanying study, or as you read your Bible, think of the women you come across as cairns. Each of them has a message for us. Each represents a time or place or person or event within the story of salvation. They each teach us something about ourselves and our place within that story. Though our names may be of little note, and our time here may be but a blink of the eye of God, we, too, are part of salvation history. We are the women who take up where the others left off. In this story of salvation, we are the nurses, judges, warriors, mothers, sinners, and evangelists. Just as the women in this book led important roles in the ancient world and the early Church, so, too, do we lead important roles in the Church today.

Saint John Paul the Great, in his Letter to Women, said, "If Christ—by his free and sovereign choice, clearly attested to by the Gospel and by the Church's constant Tradition— entrusted only to men the task of being an 'icon' of his countenance as 'shepherd' and 'bridegroom' of the Church through the exercise of the ministerial priesthood, this in no way detracts from the role of women…since all share equally in the dignity proper to the 'common priesthood' based on Baptism." [4] We are all—men and women alike—called to the common priesthood. The women highlighted in this text have been chosen so that you may come to better understand their role and yours as members of the common priesthood and in the story of salvation.

SOMETHING TO THINK ABOUT AS YOU READ

No book or study about the women of the Bible would be complete without a look at Mary and her role as the mother of Jesus, mother of the Church, and mother to all Christians. In the stories of many of the other women, you will find direct correlations to the Virgin Mary.

Saint John Paul the Great told us that "The collaboration of Christians in salvation takes place after the Calvary event, whose fruits they endeavor to spread by prayer and sacrifice. Mary, instead, co-operated during the event itself and in the role of mother; thus her co-operation embraces the whole of Christ's saving work."[5] The women of the Old Testament laid the foundation for Mary's cooperation, and the women of the New Testament continued the work of Mary in bringing her Son to the world, just as we are called to do today.

HOW TO APPROACH THIS STUDY

I recommend that you read the Bible stories about each of these women before you read the chapter. The suggested passages will be given at the beginning of each section. As you read, think about the woman in the story. Meditate on her words and actions, and put yourself in her place. Where was she from? Where was she going? What was her place in God's Salvific Plan? What can she teach you about your own faith journey and your place in God's plan? Read the Bible passages and the chapters of this book with an open heart and an open mind. Remember that you, too, are a woman of God, clothed with strength and dignity.

Amy Schisler

PART I
WOMEN OF THE OLD TESTAMENT

MOTHERING CREATION
Eve, Sarah, Rebekah, and Rebekah's Nurse, Deborah

CHAPTER ONE - EVE

To embark on a study of the women of the Bible, we must begin at the beginning. In the book of Genesis, we are introduced to two women who would become the matriarchs of creation and religion—Eve and Sarah. Our mother in creation and our mother in faith, both had a fatal flaw—lack of trust in God. Complete, faithful, and unwavering trust in God comes later, from another mother to us all, our Mother Mary.

EVE – "THE MOTHER OF ALL LIVING"
Genesis 2:18-25; Genesis 3; Genesis 4:1-16,15-26

> *Then the man said, "This at last is bone of my bones and flesh of my flesh; she shall be called Woman, because she was taken out of Man." Therefore a man leaves his father and his mother and clings to his wife, and they become one flesh.* - Genesis 2:24

Eve, whose name means, *the mother of all living*, was the first woman, the first wife, and the first mother. Eve was created because "it is not good for man to be alone. I will make a helper fit for him" (Genesis 2:18).

Eve was made from Adam, from a rib, a bone close to his heart. The Catechism states that man and woman were created "on the one hand, in perfect equality as human persons; on the other hand, in their respective beings as man and woman."[6] St. Ambrose wrote, "You are not her master, but her husband; she was not given to you to be your slave, but your wife...Reciprocate her attentiveness to you and be grateful to her for her love."[7] Eve was Adam's equal in dignity, and they were complimentary to each other. They were to be stewards of the earth in harmony with nature and God.

Unlike any of us, Eve was "constituted in an original state of holiness and justice...to share in the divine life."[8] Only one other woman ever walked this earth in an original state of holiness and justice, sharing in the divine life. Not until the Virgin Mary did we have another *Mother of all Living*. This is one of the things we should admire about Eve. She was holy, humanity's first mother, born to partake in the divine life.

Eve was blessed to share in God's plan for divine life. "Eve possessed in its fullness: security, wholeness, intimacy unmarred by shame."[9] All women are made to feel secure, to feel whole, and to be unmarred by shame. How do we achieve these

Figure A

things? By being loved securely, wholly, and without

shame. Woman was made to be loved by God and by man in an open, trusting, and holy environment.

Eve was bone of Adam's bones and was flesh of his flesh; "therefore a man leaves his father and his mother and clings to his wife, and they become one flesh" (Genesis 2:24). In becoming one flesh, Adam and Eve were living God's intended life for them, to "grow continually in their communion through day-to-day fidelity to their marriage promise of total mutual self-giving."[10] They could give totally and freely of themselves without contempt or shame or lust or any other conditions with which we must contend today. They were made only for God and for each other and lived as such…for a time.

Unfortunately, this harmony with God and each other did not last for it was Eve, the first woman, who committed the first sin—the sin of pride. Pride is "a feeling of deep pleasure or satisfaction derived from one's own achievements, the achievements of those with whom one is closely associated, or from qualities or possessions that are widely admired."[11] Pride is a sin when it is centered on what one has achieved on one's own, disregarding the role of God in the achievement, or when one derives pleasure from an admired possession in a selfish way with disregard to the needs or feelings of others.

It was not the eating of the fruit, the offering of the fruit to Adam, or the blaming of the serpent that caused the separation of human beings from God. It was Eve's pride, her desire to be "like God" (Genesis 3:5) which she felt would be achieved through the eating of the forbidden fruit. Eve admired God, but not in a reverent way. She admired what she could become if she possessed God's knowledge.

Let us not forget, though, that in the original Hebrew language in the Torah, Eve was not alone in the garden. Adam was by her side when the serpent convinced her to eat the fruit. Adam was Eve's husband, her protector. Should he not have stopped the serpent from manipulating her? For that's what happened. The serpent manipulated Eve into thinking she should not trust God, and Adam did nothing.

We are meant to protect our spouses from evil. We are meant to give each other guidance and keep each other in harmony with God. We are meant to respect and love each other unconditionally and without shame. When Adam kept silent and Eve took the fruit, they lost their innocence and their sense of equality. "The eyes of both were opened, and they knew they were naked; and they sewed fig leaves together and made themselves aprons" (Genesis 3:7). They saw each other differently, and they looked upon themselves and each other with shame.

No longer was Adam Eve's protector. On the contrary, he turned on her. Without admitting any fault of his own, he said to God, "The woman whom you gave to me, she gave me fruit of the tree, and I ate it" (Genesis 3:12). For this reason, both Adam and Eve were punished. The harmony between humans and God was replaced by a cacophony of curses for all humanity and resulted in the loss of man's trust in God and his promises.

Eve trusted the word of the serpent and faltered in the knowledge that God had given her and Adam all that was desirable—food, shelter, animal and human companions, and all the knowledge they would ever need. The serpent tricked Eve into thinking there was something she was missing, something she would only know by eating the forbidden fruit. "For God knows that when you eat of it your eyes will be opened, and you will be like God" (Genesis 3:5). He used her pride to destroy her ability to trust. She no longer trusted God but rather trusted the serpent's implication that God was withholding something from them, something she greatly desired even if she didn't know exactly what it was.

After the fall, Adam and Eve were cast out into the world and forbidden from entering the Garden of Eden. It was after this that Eve conceived and bore her sons, Cain and Abel. Eve, the mother of all living, became a mother herself. Like all mothers, she must have watched with joy as her sons grew into men, one "a keeper of sheep," and the other "a tiller of the ground" (Genesis 4:2).

Her sons were strong and successful, but one son, Cain, was a jealous and selfish man. While his brother, Abel, gave the Lord an offering of the very best and fattest of his sheep, Cain brought an offering of fruit that had fallen to the ground. When Cain saw that God was displeased with his offering but pleased with Abel's, his pride was wounded. He desired God's praise and resented his brother. In a rage, Cain killed Abel. Eve's pride and lack of trust were passed on to her son.

TRUSTING IN GOD

Eve's actions in the garden went beyond eating the apple. She not only fell to the sins of pride and distrust of God; she put the word of someone else above the word of God. She saw herself as someone who could go against God's command. She was the antithesis of Mary who trusted God completely and always kept faithful to her fiat—her yes to the angel and to God. Mary did what Eve should have done.

Does this make Eve a bad person? Does it make her someone we should despise? On the contrary, Eve is no different from you and me. She is human. She is easily fooled and tricked. She is a sinner. She is one of us.

ANOTHER CHANCE

It was through Eve that sin entered the world, through her that jealousy, rage, and death became part of the human experience. The death of her son, Abel, and the fleeing and banishment of her son, Cain (punishment for his sin), introduced Eve to another human experience—heartache. How grieved she must have been at the death and banishment of her sons. The mother of all living, because of her own actions, became the mother of none.

So many mothers are estranged from their children. So many children blame their parents for their mistakes, and many parents blame themselves for their children's mistakes. We so often try to stop our children from living their own lives because we fear their choices, their mistakes. However, it is our mistakes that make us who we are. They form us, and if we let them, they teach us.

Often, parents try to force their own life lessons on their children. Can't you imagine Eve trying to teach her boys about pride and trust? Can't you imagine her pleading with them to be better people than she and Adam were? The advice of parents often falls on deaf ears, and that is because our children need to make their own mistakes. They need to learn their own lessons. It has taken me over twenty-seven years as a parent to learn this, and I still get it wrong.

Figure B

We want to shelter our children. We want to teach them what we failed to learn at that age. We want to save them from making mistakes, but in the end, we can't know their hearts or their minds, and we can't spend our lives projecting our failings onto them.

Thankfully, our God is a loving and forgiving God. He knows that we try, and he understands that we often fail. God gave Eve a second chance and blessed her with another son, Seth. Her first two sons were lost to her, but God allowed her the chance to raise another son. "God has appointed for me another child instead of Abel, for Cain slew him" (Genesis 4:25). The Bible tells us that "Adam had other sons and daughters" before he died (Genesis 5:5). There is no mention of another wife, so we assume that this means it was Eve who gave birth to other children. The mother of all living things was given the chance to raise more sons and daughters who would go on to populate the earth.

Eve learned that God is a merciful God. He forgives. He gives us second chances, third chances, and fourth, and however many chances we need to make things right. And we are expected to do the same with others.

> Then Peter approaching asked him, "Lord, if my brother sins against me, how often must I forgive him? As many as seven times?" Jesus answered, "I say to you, not seven times but seventy-seven times" (Matthew 18:21-22)

THE NEW EVE

Because of Eve, the world was plunged into sin, thus introducing the downfall of humankind. Through the new Eve—Mary—we are given the grace of salvation. God told Adam, Eve, and the serpent, "I will put enmity between you and the woman and between your seed and her seed; he shall bruise your head, and you shall bruise his heel"

(Genesis 3:15). The seed of the woman would bruise the

head of the serpent. Mary's child, Jesus, would ultimately defeat Satan through his death on the cross.

In the moment before Jesus's death, the Apostle John is given Mary as his mother with the words, "Woman, behold your son … son, behold, your mother" (John 19:26-27). In Revelation, John refers to "A woman clothed with the sun…with child, a male child, one who is to rule all nations" (Revelations 12:1-6).

Mary, Mount St. Mary's University, Emmitsburg,

Nowhere in his gospel nor in Revelations does John refer to Mary by name. Instead, he refers to her as "woman." Eve was the one about whom God said, "She shall be called Woman" (Genesis 2:23). Eve was the first person to be called "woman" while Mary is the person referred to by Jesus and John as "Woman." Mary is the New Eve in that she is the counterpart to Jesus, the New Adam. Where Eve said no, Mary said yes. We will explore this more when we look at Mary at the Annunciation.

Eve's story is a cairn that reminds us to trust that God has given us everything we need and to always look to him when we are tempted to go astray.

CHAPTER TWO - SARAH

THE MOTHER OF NATIONS
Genesis 12; Genesis 15; Genesis 16; Genesis 17:15-21; Genesis 18:1-15; Genesis 21:1-7; Genesis 23

And God said to Abraham, "As for Sarai your wife, you shall not call her Sarai, but Sarah shall be her name. I will bless her, and moreover I will give you a son by her; I will bless her, and she shall be a mother of nations; kings of peoples shall come from her."
- Genesis 17:15-16

Sarah, the wife of Abraham, traveled with her husband when he was called by God to go to Egypt. Abraham feared that the Egyptians would be enamored of his wife's beauty and worried they would kill him and take his wife. He told her to pretend to be his sister, and she apparently agreed, perhaps affirming her deep love for her husband and desire to keep him safe; but things did not go as planned. The Pharoah took Sarah as his wife, and God sent plagues down on the house of Pharoah.

Who was this woman whom God protected with plagues? She was a woman of virtue who trusted that God would protect her, a woman who put her own life at risk to save the life of her husband. She trusted that God would keep her safe and return her to the husband who would be spared.

FROM VIRTUOUS TO DOUBTING

Unfortunately, Sarah's trust in God did not last. She wanted a child more than anything, and though God made a promise to Abraham that his descendants would be as great as the number of the stars (Genesis 15:5), Sarah continued to be childless. Sarah doubted God's word that he would fulfil her desire to conceive a child of her own, a notion that modern-day feminists might deem silly, but "continuing the lineage was the most important role women had during this time."[12]

In desperation, Sarah took matters into her own hands and gave her maid, Hagar, to Abraham so that he might have a son, as was the custom in such circumstances. Abraham agreed, dismissing the promise from God that Sarah would conceive. Sarah's offer that Abraham have a child with Hagar "seems more like a demand than a request, and the fact that Abraham listens to

Figure C

her suggests a more equal relationship than is often proposed."[13] It also suggests that Abraham was a faithful husband who, prior to this moment, had never taken another wife or a concubine as the law would have allowed for a man with a barren wife (after Sarah's death, Abraham did take another wife and had more children by concubines). In fact, according to the law, a man could divorce his wife if she failed to provide him with children after ten years of marriage. Since Abraham and Sarah were advanced in age, theirs was undoubtedly a marriage of love.

Abraham did as Sarah suggested and conceived a son, Ishmael, with her maidservant, Hagar. However, after Hagar gave birth to Ishmael, Sarah felt unloved and unworthy each time she saw her husband's child. Allowing her husband to have a child with another woman was not the same as giving him a child herself. Sarah suffered, not because of Hagar or the child, but because she went around God and his plan. She distrusted him and his promise. She thought the only way to give her husband the promised child was to find another way, another woman. She took upon herself the role of God. This led to heartbreak for both women—Sarah was tormented by Hagar, and Hagar was tormented by Sarah. Furthermore, Hagar's life was threatened by Sarah who cast out Hagar and her child from the region.

Sarah continued to pray for a child, but when the time came for the Lord to provide, Sarah's already diminished trust in God seemed to vanish altogether. Upon hearing that within a year's time, she would give birth, Sarah laughed (Genesis 18:12). Abraham and Sarah were unaware of God's power and might, and Sarah did not believe the words of the Lord nor his messengers. Like we so often do, she continued to see the world through the eyes of humans and not through the eyes of God.

So many people only see the world through the eyes of humans and not through the eyes of God. When things don't go the way that is expected, we tend to take things into our own hands. It was not enough for God to promise Abraham he would have children. Sarah had to find a way to make it happen in her time and in her way,

Figure D

and that way led to heartache, jealousy, and despair. Often, when we try to bend God's will to our own, or make things happen in our way or within our own timeframe, we end up worse off than we were before. When Sarah's own plans went awry, she laughed at the thought that God's plans would come to fruition.

NOTHING IS IMPOSSIBLE

Sarah was to bear a child at the age of ninety, according to a promise from God, but she doubted God's promise, believing she was too old to conceive. When Sarah laughed, she made the same mistake Eve made—she failed to trust God. The Lord's response was, "Is anything too hard for the Lord?" (Genesis 18:14). Several other times, particularly in the New Testament, we are told that nothing is impossible for God. Just as with Elizabeth, four-hundred-and-ninety years after Sarah, God gave a son to a woman of advanced age. When the Angel Gabriel told her cousin, Mary, that Elizabeth was with child, he assured her, "with God, nothing is impossible" (Luke 1: 37).

Sarah's lack of faith brought with it fear. After she laughed, she feared the Lord and tried to deny that she had laughed, but the Lord assured her that he had heard her. After giving birth to Isaac, Sarah said, "Who would have said to Abraham that Sarah would suckle children? Yet I have borne him a son in my old age" (Genesis 21:6). She was still surprised and marveled that God could give her a son of her own. Even after all she had witnessed, Sarah still did not have faith and trust in God.

Contrast Sarah's actions to Mary who said, "I am the handmaid of the Lord; let it be done to me according to your word" (Luke 1:38). It was not enough for Mary to say yes to the Lord. She pledged herself to his service and to his will. She accepted the word of Gabriel that she would conceive and give birth to a son and that her cousin, in her advanced age would also give birth. Mary gave herself to God so his will would be fulfilled through her.

SARAH'S JOY

I do have to wonder, though, about Sarah's reaction. When she first heard God's promise, then when she was pregnant, and again after she gave birth, Sarah was amazed by God's promise. She was further amazed by what she had done through God's miracle. Sarah then became worried that she would be the laughingstock of the tribe. Or did she? Let's take another look at what Sarah said. "Who would have said to Abraham that Sarah would suckle children? Yet I have borne him a son in my old age" (Genesis 21:6).

Perhaps Sarah wasn't afraid of being laughed at. Perhaps she was looking into the face of the babe at her breast and laughing with joy, looking forward to sharing joyous laughter with the other women about what God had done for her and through her. At the most profound moments in our lives, maybe we should laugh, allowing ourselves to marvel at the workings of God. Saint John Paul the Great once remarked, "Joy is the infallible sign of God's presence." Perhaps Sarah's laughter was nothing more than a sign of her joy and acknowledgment of God's presence. Look for moments of joy, times when you purposefully recognize all that God has done for you. These are cairns that will help us stay faithful to the Lord.

THE DEATH OF SARAH

Sarah's faith was tested just as our faith is tested. Her story reminds us that even those who trust in God can fail the test. Still, Sarah's faith was restored, and she remained faithful to God. Like the Biblical Patriarchs, she lived to an old age, and her death was recorded in the Torah, one of the few women to have her death mentioned in the scriptures at all. Not only was it mentioned, but Genesis 23 gives a highly detailed account of her death and burial. Abraham "went in to mourn for Sarah and to weep for her" (Genesis 23:2) and then gave a great exhortation to the Hittites, occupiers of the land of Hebron in Canaan, asking them to give him the field on which his wife was entombed. "The field and the cave that is in it were made over to Abraham as a possession for a burying place by the Hittites" (Genesis 23:20). To this day, Sarah is buried in the Cave of the Patriarchs with her husband, son, and grandson (Genesis 49:31).

We, too, sometimes laugh when we think something is impossible. Like Sarah and Abraham, we become afraid that what we want won't happen or that we've offended God. We, too, place our trust in ourselves or others instead of God. Like Eve and Sarah, when we fail, we must seek God's mercy. Nothing is impossible with God. We must trust in him and his plan for our lives.

> "Watch and pray that you may not undergo the test. The spirit is willing, but the flesh is weak" (Matthew 26:41).

CHAPTER THREE - REBEKAH

Genesis 24; Genesis 25:19-34; Genesis 26:34-35; Genesis 27

THE MOTHER OF THOUSANDS OF TEN THOUSANDS

And they blessed Rebekah, and said to her, "Our sister, be the mother of thousands of ten thousands; and may your descendants possess the gate of those who hate them." - Genesis 24: 60

Rebekah became the wife of Isaac, the son of Sarah and Abraham, and thus became the new matriarch of the Chosen People. It is written in Genesis that Rebekah was "very fair" (Genesis 15:16) and showed great kindness to Isaac's servant who was sent to find him a wife from among Isaac's kin. She gave water to the servant and his camels and took him home with her to her father's house for the night. The servant knew immediately this was the right woman for his master. He was proven correct, for Rebekah and Isaac loved each other at once. They married and left to dwell in the land of Isaac's father. Rebekah's sisters were distressed that she was leaving so suddenly, but she insisted, showing her deep love for Isaac, her trust in God, and her own independence.

Like her mother-in-law, Rebekah had trouble conceiving and waited twenty years before giving birth to twins, Jacob and Esau. From all that is written, it seems that Rebekah and Isaac had a good marriage, one of love and trust. So, how did it go wrong?

REBEKAH HEARS GOD'S PLAN

Despite her kindness and her seemingly good marriage, Rebekah has been known for many generations of Christians as a woman of deceit; however, our Jewish brothers and sisters do not see Rebekah this way. When it came time for Isaac, who was sick in bed, to bless his eldest son, Esau, Rebekah convinced their younger son, Jacob, to trick his father into bestowing the blessing on him. Rebekah's story, according to many Christians, has always been one of a mother choosing one son over the other and helping him to lie and trick his ailing father.

However, when Rebekah conceived the twins, the Lord said to her, "Two nations are in your womb, and two peoples, born of you, shall be

Figure E

divided; the one shall be stronger than the other; the elder shall serve the younger" (Genesis 25:23). Before we go on, let's take a moment to think about this. God spoke to Adam about his role in creation and God's plan for humankind. Later, God made a covenant with Abraham, sharing his plans for Abraham's descendants. Here, God shared his plans with Rebekah, a woman, someone who would have been held in low esteem during that time. What great faith and what a beautiful relationship she must have had with the Lord! What a beautiful statement for all women that God transcends status and gender barriers and speaks to us! This is the Rebekah that our Jewish brothers and sisters know and love.

Perhaps Rebekah, like Mary, kept these words in her heart, pondering them as she watched her boys grow into men. Perhaps she knew that she was doing the will of God, cooperating with his plan, by making sure Jacob received the blessing and the inheritance that tradition held belonged to his brother, Esau. "This use of deception should not be understood as indicative of a woman's

Figure F

nature but instead the method a marginalized people have to resort to in order to serve justice and God's purpose."[14]

The Bible tells us that Isaac loved Esau, and Rebekah loved Jacob, but was Rebekah deceitful because of that love? It is Rebekah who "sets off the chain of events which will ensure the right son inherits the covenant. Though her plan employs deception, she remains dedicated to both her family and to God."[15] She goes even further, telling Jacob that she will take any future curse for their actions upon herself. She will take responsibility for what Jacob does.

After the deception of Isaac, Rebekah learns of Esau's anger and implores Jacob to flee until his brother is ready to forgive him. She laments, "Why should I be bereft of you both in one day?" (Genesis 27:45). She knows she has lost one son to anger and does not want to lose the other to death. This is a mother who loves both her sons. Before Jacob leaves, Rebekah ensures that Esau's father properly blesses him. She then attempts to ensure that both sons marry the right women—women who will be faithful to the God of Abraham.

RECOGNIZING GOD'S PLAN

Rebekah knew of God's plan and used her abilities and intellect to make sure it happened. Was she taking matters into her own hands and asserting her own will? Certainly, it could be viewed as such, unless we consider the fact that God shared his plan with her. He told her which son was to lead his people. Rebekah could have ignored God's plan. She could have allowed Isaac to bless Esau, but she understood that God's vision was greater than her own.

How easy it is to fall into the trap of doing things the way we think they should be done rather than how God wants them to be done. How easy it is to give in to temptation like Eve or laugh at God's promises like Sarah. If only these women had had the wisdom of Solomon and the faith of Sirach, who perhaps learned from those who came before them. For Solomon wrote, "He who

> **He who trusts in his own mind is a fool; but he who walks in wisdom will be delivered. (Proverbs 28:26).**

trusts in his own mind is a fool; but he who walks in wisdom will be delivered" (Proverbs 28:26), and Sirach taught,

> Trust in him, and he will help you; make your ways straight, and hope in him. You who fear the Lord, trust in him, and your reward will not fail; Consider the ancient generations and see: who ever trusted in the Lord and was put to shame? Or whoever persevered in the fear of the Lord and was forsaken? Or whoever called upon him and was overlooked? Woe to the faint heart, for it has no trust! Therefore it will not be sheltered (Sirach 2:6, 8, 10, 13).

It seems that Rebekah had Solomon's wisdom and was not faint of heart. She knew what she had to do, and she followed the will of God the only way she could. She believed in God's plan and helped put it into motion.

"NOT AS I WILL, BUT AS YOU WILL" (MATTHEW 26:39)

It is often easier to trust our own judgment, to take matters into our own hands, and to make things happen along our own timeline. In his book, *Catholicism*, Bishop Robert Barron likens God's plan to Georges Seurat's pointillist masterpiece, *Sunday Afternoon on the Island of La Grande Jatte*. If you stand too close, you will "see only a collection of meaningless blotches, but as you step back the points begin to blend and figures, groups, and patterns emerge. Only when you view it from the far side of the room does the painting disclose itself as a gorgeously harmonic unity. God is like an artist, and his canvas is the whole of space and time." [16] His plan is much bigger, much more encompassing, and much more beautiful than we could ever imagine from our close and unknowing perspective.

Figure G

God's plan depended upon Jacob being the master over Esau. If that was the case, then why was Esau born first? Why wasn't Jacob the true heir from the beginning? Perhaps God wanted to use Rebekah to teach us something.

Rebekah's actions are a cairn teaches us that God's plan is perfect, and that often, he will call on us to help him achieve it. He does not need us to take matters into our hands, but he wills our compliance, our collaboration, our trust. We must submit to his will even if we think our way is better. In the words of Jesus, "not as I will, but as you will" (Matthew 26:39).

If we try to interfere with God's plan, we turn his masterpiece into no more than a paint-by-number page on which we choose our own colors rather than following the guide. In those times, we should take a step back and try to see God's brushstrokes, to hear his voice. Rebekah did hear God's voice, pondering their meaning for many years until she understood why God had shared his plan with her. She knew that God had chosen the younger brother, Jacob, just as he had chosen her father-in-law, Isaac, the younger brother of Ishmael. By listening to God's word, pondering it in her heart, and waiting for the right time, Rebekah was able to collaborate in God's plan for her son and for their people.

Like Rebekah, we are sometimes called to aid God in his plan. Through prayer and the careful cultivation of an intimate relationship with God, like Rebekah, we can hear the voice of God sharing his plans with us. We can cooperate with God to further his kingdom on earth and in Heaven. To do that, though, we must trust God and forge an intimate relationship with him. Only through contemplative prayer can we clearly see God's masterpiece and our role in the story.

REBEKAH'S NURSE, DEBORAH

Genesis 24:52-61; Genesis 35:5-8

And Deborah, Rebekah's nurse, died, and she was buried under an oak below Bethel; so the name of it was called Allon-bacuth.
- Genesis 35:8

A WOMAN OF MYSTERY

Who was Rebekah's nurse? Mentioned twice in Genesis and only once by name, Deborah was Rebekah's nurse but not the same Deborah we will meet later in Judges. The Deborah of Genesis held the position of nurse, but it is unknown whether she was Rebekah's own nurse since childhood, or if she was the nursemaid who helped Rebekah care for and breastfeed Jacob and Esau, or if both nurses were one in the same.

Deborah's name means *honey*. Is it a coincidence that we see her once, anonymously, when Rebekah gives birth, and then once more, by name, at the hour of her death when Jacob and his family enter the promised *Land of Milk and Honey*?

We know nothing about the death of Isaac's wife, Rebekah, other than where she is buried—in the Cave of the

Patriarchs with her husband and son. We don't even know when she died. How strange it is, then, that we are told of the death of her nurse, Deborah. Add to that the fact that Deborah's death is mentioned in the middle of the return of Rebekah's son, Jacob, from his exile, and we have quite the Biblical riddle. No wonder scholars have a hard time deciphering her role in the family.

Does her presence along Jacob's journey mean that Deborah was with Jacob on his travels? Jewish scholars believe that Rebekah sent Deborah to Jacob to help raise his children.[17] Did she go to Bethel after the death of Rebekah, or had she been with Jacob all the years he was away from Canaan or just when he married and had children? Was she there when he met Rachel at the well? Why is this small fact about his mother's nurse the first mention of death in all of Jacob's story? Her death was greatly lamented, and there was much weeping, so much that the place of her burial was named, Allon-Bacuth—*Oak of Weeping*—indicating she died among people who loved her.[18] Who was she that the people mourned for her like this, and why was it recorded in scripture?

Scripture tells us this place where the oak stood and where Deborah was buried was "below Bethel." It was near Bethel that Jacob wrestled with God and erected a monument to him. Just after this, a monument was erected for his mother's nurse over her tomb, a cairn if you will. One scholar so beautifully said, "Deborah did not utter a single word in the Jacob Cycle, but her voice could be heard in the weeping of Jacob's household - and in the whisper of the terebinth tree."[19]

When I began writing this book, it was pointed out to me by my parish priest that I was receiving signs in threes. He felt this was very meaningful since, in his words, "God sends us signs in groups of three." In addition to that, I've been told many times during my life, and bore witness myself, to the idiom that death comes in threes. How interesting, then, that Deborah's death was the first of three reported in Genesis 35. The other two were Isaac's and Rachel's. Isaac was Rebekah's husband and Jacob's father while Rachel was Jacob's wife. As with Deborah, a memorial was erected over Rachel's tomb.

Is there a meaning to Deborah's death being the first of three? Could her death, which took place along Jacob's journey, have been a symbol that something important was happening, something that brought harmony and wholeness to Jacob's story?

We are told that Rachel died on their way to Bethlehem and then "Jacob came to his father Isaac at Mamre where Abraham and Isaac had sojourned…And Isaac breathed his last…and his sons Esau and Jacob buried him" (Genesis 35: 27-29). After the death of these three, Jacob stopped journeying, and the story of his son, Joseph began. Perhaps these deaths signify that this chapter in salvation history has reached its conclusion, and the family of Isaac and Jacob has been made whole again. Harmony has been restored, and God is present with Jacob and his people.

THE NUMBER THREE

The number 3 symbolizes harmony and wholeness and represents the presence of God, the spiritual realm. Creation was divided into two sets of 3 days, each day of creation told of 3 things created, Jonah spent 3 days in the belly of the great fish. There were 3 magi and 3 gifts, and 3 members of the "inner circle" (Peter, James, and John). Satan offered Jesus 3 temptations, Jesus prayed 3 times in the Garden of Gethsemane, and Peter denied Christ 3 times. Jesus's cross was one of 3, Jesus died at 3:00, darkness covered the land for 3 hours, he spent 3 days in the tomb, and of course, there is the Trinity. These are but a few of the occurrences of the number three in the Bible.

DEBORAH'S PURPOSE

The truth is, we will never know any more about Deborah than the facts that she was Rebekah's nurse (Genesis 24:59), was known to Jacob (Genesis 35:8), and died near Bethel in the company of people who loved her (Genesis 35:8). For most people throughout time, that is the case. We live, we care for others, we have friends and family, we are loved, and we die. There will be little more said about most of us than those few things.

However, we are all children of God. We all have a purpose and a mission. Deborah helped Rebekah deliver Jacob and Esau and probably helped Rebekah nurse the twins as babies. Some scholars believe she was Rebekah's teacher and then taught Jacob and Esau. [20] Maybe she packed Jacob's bag when he fled. Perhaps she went with him, a gift from his mother so that he had a mother-figure to look out for him and see to his needs.

Aren't we, as women, called to do all those things? We are called to give life in some way, through our own pregnancies or through helping other women or by bringing to life a cause, an event, or mission for God. We are called to help others who are in need and to look out for each other. Saint John Paul the Great, in *Mulieris Dignitatem* said, "Spiritual motherhood takes on many different forms...it can express itself as concern for people, especially the neediest: the sick, the handicapped, the abandoned, orphans, the elderly, children, young people, the imprisoned and, in general, people on the edges of society."[21]

Like Deborah, we are called to take care of God's people. "For I was hungry and you gave me food, I was thirsty and you gave me drink, a stranger and you welcomed me, naked and you clothed me, ill and you cared for me, in prison and you visited me... Amen, I say to you, whatever you did for one of these least brothers of mine, you did for me" (Matthew 25:35-36).

> "Amen, I say to you, whatever you did for one of these least brothers of mine, you did for me" (Matthew 25:36).

Deborah was faceless and was nameless except for one small passage. Yet the impact she must have had on Rebekah and Jacob was tremendous. As a nurse, a friend, a second mother, a caregiver, and a companion, she would have fed, clothed, cared for, taught, and visited. She did what we are meant to do. Even if nobody ever knows our names, may those who know us find reason for great weeping at our passing.

DOING GOD'S WORK
Rachel, Leah, the Midwives, and Miriam

CHAPTER FOUR - RACHEL AND LEAH

Genesis 29; Genesis 30; Genesis 31; Genesis 35:16-26; Genesis 37:5-11

ROMANCE AND SORROW

So Jacob went in to Rachel also, and he loved Rachel more than Leah. - Genesis 29:30

There are many stories throughout the Bible of husbands taking wives, but none have the romantic fervor of the story of Rachel and Jacob. Imagine journeying many miles to an unknown land to find your kinfolk and seek a wife.

Imagine experiencing love at first sight when the woman of your dreams, one "beautiful and lovely" (Genesis 29:17), greets you upon your arrival at the well. Imagine pledging your

Figure 11

love to her, securing her hand in marriage after seven years of labor as an indentured servant, then awaking the day after your wedding to find that your father-in-law replaced your beloved with her sister.

Thus was the beginning of the love story of Jacob and Rachel. There's an old saying, what goes around comes around. Jacob and his brother, Esau, were at odds with each other. Like Cain and Abel, like Isaac and Ishmael, and like Jacob and Esau, Jacob's wives, Rachel and Leah, experienced sibling rivalry, not because of their own actions, but because of the actions of their parents. Though done for the right reasons, as we have already explored, Jacob and his mother, Rebekah, deceived Isaac and Esau. After fleeing from his brother, Jacob met and fell in love with Rachel, but Rachel's father, Laban, deceived Jacob and forced him to labor for another seven years so they could marry. The rivalries between Jacob and Laban, Rachel and Leah, and eventually between Jacob's sons, had long lasting effects. These complex relationships gave rise to the Twelve Tribes of Israel but also led to the enslavement of their nation at the hands of the Egyptians.[*]

While Jacob labored for seven years, Rachel watched as he and Leah bore children and formed a family. Watching her beloved with her sister, day after day, waiting for her time to come, must have been excruciatingly painful for Rachel. God's people waited four-thousand years for the Messiah. David wrote, "I wait for the Lord, my whole being waits,

---

[*] Rachel bore Joseph, Issacs's beloved son, who was sold into slavery by his brothers. After reconciling, Joseph's family immigrated to Egypt and became slaves of Pharoah until Moses led their descendants into the Promised Land.

and in his word, I put my hope. I wait for the Lord more than watchmen wait for the morning, more than watchmen wait for the morning" (Psalm 130:5-7). We all wait, sometimes in vain, but having patience is essential to the holy life. St. Augustine said, "patience is the companion of wisdom." When we wait for something or someone, when we hold fast to that desire over time, when we understand that patience is part of the process, we reap great rewards.

---

7 – The Number of Completion

The number seven is significant. It took seven days for God to create the earth. It is seen as the number of completeness or perfection. Every seven years, the Israelites canceled all debts owed and freed their slaves (Deuteronomy 15:1-2). After seven years, Jacob married Leah, and after another seven, his debt for his marriage to Rachel was paid.

It is no coincidence that Jacob had to serve seven years after he fled his home and arrived at the home of his kinfolk. Jacob had to atone for the deception he committed at the urging of his mother. Complete and perfect atonement for his mother's deception was reached after seven years, but Jacob, complicit in the act of deceit, must spend another seven years atoning for his own sin. Even if Rebekah acted as God's partner, Isaac was still deceived, and atonement was necessary for Jacob to move on.

FROM HEARTACHE TO JOY

Rachel must have suffered unbearable heartache after learning of the marriage of her sister to her beloved, Jacob. "These two, who tended flocks, baked the bread, wove the tents, and drew the water for their families side by side their whole lives, also vied for the attention of the same man."[22]

To make matters worse, Leah conceived and bore Jacob four sons while Rachel was unable to conceive. Though they met at the well where Rachel drew water, a symbol of life, Rachel could bear no life within her womb.

Like Sarah, Rachel gave her maidservant to her husband, and she gave him two sons. The first, Rachel named Naphtali, meaning *wrestling* and states, "I have had a great struggle with my sister" (Genesis 30:8).

Figure 1

Not to be outdone in this game of sibling rivalry, Leah gave her maidservant to Jacob, who also gave Jacob two sons. Leah then gave birth to another son and a daughter while Rachel was forced to watch her husband with his eleven children—ten boys and one girl—none of them hers.

"Then God remembered Rachel, and God hearkened to her and opened her womb" (Genesis 30:22). This son and the next, became Jacob's pride and joy. He loved them above all the others because they came from the womb of his beloved Rachel. She and Jacob waited seven years only to be deceived, then even longer for Rachel to conceive. How great was their joy when Joseph was born! The longer we must wait for something, the greater the joy we find in receiving it.

A FAMILY ON THE MOVE

After Rachel and Leah had been married to Jacob for some time, long enough to have had twelve children, including Joseph and their sister, Dinah, Jacob realized that his father-in-law and brothers-in-law were jealous of his success with his lands and livestock. The Lord told Jacob to return to the land of his father, so Jacob called his wives together and told them of his plan to take his family and return home to the land of Canaan and the loving arms of his father, Isaac. Rachel and Leah answered him, "whatever God has said to you, do" (Genesis 31:16).

It sounds simple to say that they packed up and moved back to Jacob's hometown. They just needed to throw their things into some boxes, tear down their tents, and load up their camels, right? Not quite. Jacob had amassed an enormous amount of cattle. Between Rachel, Leah, and their maidservants, there were twelve children to look after. They did not know if Jacob's brother, Esau, still wanted to kill Jacob for stealing his birthright. They had a five-hundred-mile journey ahead of them, and Rachel was pregnant with her second child.

Despite the dangers, hardships, and fear of the unknown, the sisters placed their trust in Jacob and, more importantly, in God. They packed their things, climbed onto their camels, and headed out toward an unfamiliar land. The women must have been in constant fear. They left their family, sneaking away in the night for fear that

their own kin would try to stop or
harm them. They were traveling far
to a strange place. Their children
were, no doubt, tired and hungry
on the journey, perhaps frightened
themselves. Rachel and Leah may
have been rivals for the love of

Figure J

their husband, but they were wives and mothers. While on
this journey, their tasks of taking care of their families
would not have changed. They still needed to plan meals,
wash clothes, and keep tabs on their children. Leah and the
maidservants probably had to do even more work to care
for all the children as well as Rachel, who was pregnant.

During this time, Rachel went into labor and gave birth to
Benjamin, but she had complications during labor. "As her
soul was departing (for she died), she called his name Ben-
oni, but his father called his name Benjamin" (Genesis
35:18). Ben-oni means, *Son of my sorrow*, and Benjamin
means, *Son of the right hand*.[23] Rachel was nearing death,
leaving her beloved husband and her children in the hands
of her sister, and her pain and sorrow must have been great.
Perhaps Jacob's naming of their son was a tribute to his
true love, the wife who was his right hand in life, the one
for whom he had worked a total of fourteen years to wed.

To this day, there is a Jewish tradition in which a woman ties
a red string around Rachel's tomb seven times—the number
of completion—and then wears the string to ensure
fertility.[24] Rachel's tomb is a cairn for the Jewish people – a
reminder of the promises of God.

RACHEL'S LEGACY

Through all the loss and heartache—the marriage of Jacob to her sister, the years when she could not conceive, the leaving behind of her loved ones at God's command to uproot their family, the moving to and from multiple lands until Rachel went into labor, and her death after giving birth to Benjamin—Rachel remained faithful to her husband, their sons, and God. She was rewarded by God with many generations of offspring through Joseph and Benjamin.

Rachel's legacy is that of the prayerful mother. As Jacob's wife, she would have been a true mother and mother-by-marriage to the Twelve Tribes of Israel. Their children would have been her grandchildren, and so on. In effect, she and Leah were the mothers of the all the tribes of Israel just as Jacob was the father of the tribes.* In the book of Jeremiah, Rachel was said to have wept for the fate of her children—the children of Israel—during the Babylonian Exile, when the Israelites were forced from the Promised Land.

> Thus says the LORD: In Ramah is heard the sound of sobbing, bitter weeping! Rachel mourns for her children, she refuses to be consoled for

---

* God changed Jacob's name to Israel, and his twelve sons became the patriarchs of the Israelites. When the Promised Land was divided amongst the people, it was divided according to the families that descended from each of the sons of Jacob—the Twelve Tribes of Israel. (Joshua 13)

her children—they are no more! Thus says the LORD: Cease your cries of weeping, hold back your tears! There is compensation for your labor—oracle of the LORD—they shall return from the enemy's land (Jeremiah 31:15-16).

The mother who wept because she was initially unable to bear children, wept for those children throughout her life, and continues to weep for them and their offspring in death. Her tomb is a place to pray and plead for the sons and daughters of Israel. Like all mothers, Rachel loved her children and prayed for their safety. Like Mary, who wept for her son as he hung on the cross and weeps for us today,[25] Rachel still weeps for her children.

Rachel's Weeping

Jewish texts conclude that Rachel died before Joseph was sold into slavery by his brothers. The Midrash, an ancient Hebrew text, says Joseph was the first person to cry at his mother's tomb. When he was being taken away to Egypt after being sold into slavery, the story goes, he broke away from the caravan and ran to his mother's grave. He threw himself down and wept loudly, calling to his mother to wake up and see his suffering. His mother heard him and said, "Do not fear. Go with them, and God will be with you."[26] God was indeed with him. He protected Joseph from harm, gave him the gift of dream interpretation, elevated him to be the trusted right hand of the pharaoh, and reunited him with his father and brothers. Joseph became one of the greatest prophets of Israel.

WHAT ABOUT LEAH?

Let us not forget Leah, who suffered as well. With each child she bore, she begged God to let her husband love her as he loved her sister. She tried over and over to win his affection, and she, too, stayed true to Jacob and God. Was Leah ever happy? Did Jacob come to love her more after Rachel's death when Leah became mother to Rachel's sons? Jacob referred to Leah as "your mother" when Joseph told his father about his dream (Genesis 37:10). Perhaps he came to see her faithfulness and her love for him and their children. How difficult it must have been for her, all those years, waiting to be recognized by her husband, waiting to feel his love and affection outside of procreation.

There are many women today who wait, who pray, who beg God to open their husband's eyes. There are many who still feel the sting of their husbands' choosing another woman or pornography or alcohol or any number of vices. Certainly, Leah felt ugly, ashamed, unwanted, unloved, and unseen, but she waited and had faith, and she was rewarded.

It is not Rachel but Leah who is buried in the Cave of the Patriarchs where Jacob joined her after death. "There they buried Abraham and Sarah; there they buried Isaac and Rebekah his wife; and there I buried Leah" (Genesis 49:31). Leah rests with her husband, the man she loved and waited for so long for him to love her back. Furthermore, God rewarded Leah with the greatest blessing—her son, Judah, was the head of the tribe whose line of descendancy led to David, Israel's greatest king, and then to Jesus. It was through the offspring of Leah, the wife rejected by her husband in life but adjoined to him after death, that we were given the Messiah.

CHAPTER FIVE - SHIPHRAH, PUAH, AND MIRIAM - THE WOMEN OF EXODUS

THE ISRAELITE MIDWIVES IN EGYPT
Exodus 1

The midwives, however, feared God, and did not do as the king of Egypt commanded them, but let the male children live.
- Exodus 1:17

After the death of Rachel, Jacob's family migrated to Egypt to join Joseph who had been sold into slavery but gained freedom and prestige in the land of the pharaoh. Eventually, Joseph's high regard was forgotten, but his descendants in Egypt were fruitful and multiplied. The Egyptians began to fear this growing community, so Pharoah made them slaves to Egypt and "made the sons of Israel serve with rigor, and made their lives bitter with hard service in mortar and in brick, and in all kinds of work in the field" (Exodus 1:13-14). When the Israelites proved too strong to become subservient even through hard manual labor, Pharoah instructed the midwives to kill all male babies upon birth to weaken the people of Israel. When Pharoah decided to rid his country of the Israelites, he began "with the existing structure of authority and power within the Hebrews—the midwives. The midwives literally have power over life and death."[27] The midwives were to abort the babies during delivery.

The leaders of the midwives, Shiphrah—meaning able to make something better—and Puah—meaning a gift of speech, refused to do as Pharoah commanded. They allowed the male babies to live because "they feared God" (Exodus 1:17). The wording of the verse, "allowing the boys to live" (1:18) suggests that the women not only saved the boys from death but gave them whatever they needed to live, including food and water.

Why did Pharoah single out the boys and not the girls? The boys would grow to be soldiers, but many of the girls would inter- marry, convert, and give worship to the Egyptians gods, and bring forth Egyptian children. The girls were needed for the continuance of the Egyptians, but the boys

Figure K

were dangerous and needed to be killed. "The Egyptians consider women harmless; they are useful for having more children and building up their nation. Yet...the Hebrew women are robust and strong... And the midwives are not subservient."[28] When questioned by Pharoah, the women told him, "The Hebrew women are not like the Egyptian women; for they are vigorous and are delivered before the midwife comes to them" (Exodus 1:19). In other words, they led Pharoah to believe that the Hebrew women gave birth quickly before the midwives could intervene. Their trickery allowed the Israelites to continue populating. The Midrash* tells us that the two women prayed to God to preserve all the babies, even those who might have died of natural causes. They did not want Pharoah's plan to kill the babies to have any success.

Through women like Shiphrah and Puah, God protected both the midwives and the babies of Israel, and the people grew in strength and number. Every male Israelite who survived this time was saved by these women. The acts of Shiphrah and Puah were nothing short of heroic. If it had become known to Pharoah that they were preserving the lives of the babies they were ordered to kill, the women would have faced death themselves. What courage they must have had! The midwives "symbolize birth, deliverance, freedom, life, truth, passage…They bring forth life, they liberate, they mediate between one world and another, they comfort."[29] Shiphrah and Puah saved lives, innocent babies' lives, and "God dealt well with the midwives" (Exodus 1:20.

It takes great courage to stand up against authority or against society, yet God sometimes calls us to do just that. Ostracization, ridicule, or even death could result from someone going against orders or against the grain. These midwives lived what Jeremiah would later proclaim, and what we are called to do, "Thus says the Lord, do justice and righteousness…And do no wrong…nor shed innocent

---

* The Midrash is a compilation of textual interpretations of the Torah by Judaic authorities.

blood in this place" (Jeremiah 22:3). These women saved the lives of babies in a culture of death. Where are the brave women of our time who will stand up and do the same? Surely, they are the women who work at pregnancy centers, those who protest at clinics and in front of courthouses, those who carry babies against the odds, and those who lovingly care for the sick and elderly.

We are called to act for justice and speak for the unborn, the orphans, the homeless, the condemned, the elderly, the disabled, and anyone who needs protection. We are to be like Shiphrah and Puah, courageous and unyielding, ready to do what we must to help those who have nobody else to help them. We are called to rally against the culture of death and save all lives that need to be saved.

Some modern scholars believe Shiphrah and Puah to have been the first Jewish converts, women of Egyptian or other Gentile ethnicity, who saved the Hebrew people. Based on notes in the Talmud*, other modern-day Jewish scholars believe Shiphrah to have been the mother of Moses, known as Jochebed. Her courageous deeds made her the matriarch of all the Israelites whom Moses led from slavery. The Talmud also identifies Puah as Miriam, who as a child helped her mother as the midwife's assistant and then carried her mother's own child, Moses, to the Nile to save him from death.

---

* The Talmud is a collection of Rabbinic notes on the scriptures.

MIRIAM - THE FIRST PROPHETESS
Exodus 2:1-10; Exodus 14; Exodus 15:1-21; Numbers 12; Numbers 20: 1-2

Then his sister said to Pharaoh's daughter, "Shall I go and call you a nurse from the Hebrew women to nurse the child for you?" And Pharaoh's daughter said to her, "Go." So the girl went and called the child's mother. - Exodus 2:7-8

Miriam, the sister of Aaron and Moses, has some sober lessons to teach us. She knew what it was to experience hope and despair, terror and deliverance, slavery and freedom, unimportance and prominence. She was a good example, and she was a bad example; in fact, she was just like we are! We are not perfect every day of every month of every year and most likely will not reach perfection at any point in our earthly lives. God is so gracious with us, so patient, and so forgiving—but there are times when a loving, Heavenly Father must act with decisive discipline, lest the course we have chosen destroys us and all those who look to us for leadership and guidance. This was the case with Miriam.

Miriam's first official appearance in the Bible is in Exodus 2:4 when Moses's sister carries the basket with the babe inside and sets it on its course on the Nile. The sister is not named and could be someone other than Miriam, but the genealogies mentioned in Numbers 26:59 and 1 Chronicles 6:3 only mention Moses, Aaron, and Miriam as the children of Amram. Going with the Jewish teaching that the older sister is, in fact, Miriam, we can see that she played an important role in saving the life of her brother, the greatest prophet of Israel. Perhaps Miriam's "gift of speech," which persuaded Pharaoh's daughter to allow her mother to nurse the babe, is why Jewish scholars believe she and Puah were the same person.

Like Rebekah, Miriam played an important part in God's plan. Through her intercession, Moses was saved, and thus was able to save his people. How are we called to help further God's plan? How can we intercede on the part of the others? How are we, sisters in Christ, being called to help our fellow sisters and brothers?

THE SAVIOR BECOMES THE SAVED

Then Miriam, the prophetess, the sister of Aaron, took a timbrel in her hand; and all the women went out after her with timbrels and dancing. - Exodus 15:20

We see Miriam next when she leads the women in dance after the Israelites safely make it through the parted Red Sea. It is in this passage that Miriam is referred to as "the prophetess" (Exodus 15:20). Miriam, at her brother's side, encouraged the people to listen to Moses, to follow him, and to praise God for their escape from the Egyptians. It should not surprise any of us that Miriam, who saved the lives of babies and held persuasion over Pharaoh's daughter, aided her brother in leading their people from Egypt.

Miriam had not seen her brother for many years. Once exiled, he married, had children, and led a prosperous life while his family was enslaved. For all the intervening years between setting her brother afloat in the Nile and the exodus from Egypt, Miriam lived in slavery, knowing all the time that her brother had been spared and raised as the heir to the Egyptian throne and was then cast out of Egypt into the desert. Imagine her shock at Moses's reappearance after his exile in the desert and his claims that he had been sent by God to rescue his people.

Miriam could have resented Moses. She could have accused him of turning his back on his family and their people. She could have convinced the people not to listen to him. Instead, she stood by him, giving us all a wonderful example of trusting in God and in those whom He sends. How strong her faith must have been. What wonder she must have felt, not only as a slave and sister of the man who had come to free her, but as the child who secured her brother's own life. The savior had become the saved. Then Miriam, a lowly slave, moved beyond her status in life to become a leader among her people.

Moses, Aaron, and Miriam led the people from Egypt, across the desert, to the Red Sea. The siblings were given three gifts, one each, and Miriam's gift was a well that provided water for the people.[30] Much like Rachel and Leah, Miriam trusted God and trusted her brother to lead them to safety. According to the Midrash, Moses led the men out of Egypt and taught them Torah, and Miriam led the women and taught them.[31]

After passing through the Red Sea, the people praised God in song. Though this song is identified in Exodus as The Song of Moses, with only one stanza attributed to Miriam, historical and

Figure L.

literary studies by Jewish scholars tells us the entire song was Miriam's.[32] She walked with her brother as he led their people out of bondage, and she led the women in song and dance. This is the first song in scripture, and it was sung by a woman. How beautiful that a woman led other women singing the first song of praise to God.

Miriam, who was obviously musically inclined, was moved to sing and dance. This is not the only time we will see this. Deborah the Judge and Hannah, mother of Samuel, will both sing and dance before the Lord. King David "danced before the Lord with all his might" (2 Samuel 6:14). And what is the Magnificat of Mary if not a song of praise (Luke 1:46-56)? Jewish scholar, David Winship wrote,

> A holy melody has the power to bring one to the level of prophecy. Music is the foundation of true attachment to God. Music has a tremendous power to draw you to God. Get into the habit of always singing a tune. It will give you a new life and send joy into your soul. Then you will be able to bind yourself to God.[33]

THE SONG OF MIRIAM

I will sing to the Lord, for he is gloriously triumphant; horse and chariot he has cast into the sea.

My strength and my refuge is the Lord, and he has become my savior. This is my God, I praise him; the God of my father, I extol him. The Lord is a warrior, Lord is his name!

Pharaoh's chariots and army he hurled into the sea; the elite of his officers were drowned in the Red Sea. The flood waters covered them, they sank into the depths like a stone. Your right hand, O Lord, magnificent in power, your right hand, O Lord, shattered the enemy.

In your great majesty you overthrew your adversaries; you loosed your wrath to consume them like stubble.

At the blast of your nostrils the waters piled up, the flowing waters stood like a mound, the flood waters foamed in the midst of the sea.

The enemy boasted, "I will pursue and overtake them; I will divide the spoils and have my fill of them; I will draw my sword; my hand will despoil them!"

When you blew with your breath, the sea covered them; like lead they sank in the mighty waters.

Who is like you among the gods, O Lord? Who is like you, magnificent among the holy ones? Awe-inspiring in deeds of renown, worker of wonders, when you stretched out your right hand, the earth swallowed them!

In your love you led the people you redeemed; in your strength you guided them to your holy dwelling.

The peoples heard and quaked; anguish gripped the dwellers in Philistia. Then were the chieftains of Edom dismayed, the nobles of Moab seized by trembling; All the inhabitants of Canaan melted away; terror and dread fell upon them.

By the might of your arm they became silent like stone, while your people, Lord, passed over, while the people whom you created passed over.

You brought them in, you planted them on the mountain that is your own—The place you made the base of your throne, Lord, the sanctuary, Lord, your hands established. May the Lord reign forever and ever!

Sing to the Lord, for he is gloriously triumphant; horse and chariot he has cast into the sea.

Exodus 15:1-18, 21

How often do we feel so much joy that we find ourselves singing and dancing? In those moments, do we echo the words of Miriam, "I will sing to the Lord, for he is gloriously triumphant" (Exodus 15:21)? How well do we use the talents the Lord has given to us to do his will or to praise his name?

BETRAYAL AND REDEMPTION

And the anger of the Lord was kindled against them, and he departed; and when the cloud removed from over the tent, behold, Miriam was leprous, as white as snow. - Numbers 12:9-10

In Numbers, we see Miriam turning on God. She turned on the Lord and on her brothers. First, "Miriam and Aaron spoke against Moses on the pretext of the Cushite woman he had married; for he had in fact married a Cushite woman" (Numbers 12:1). This could refer to Moses's wife, Zipporah, a native of Midian who Jewish scholars tell us was dark-skinned, or to a new wife, possibly of African (Cushite) descent. The Bible does not specify whom the wife was nor if Zipporah was still alive at this point. The comment could have been a reference to his wife's goodness or her skin color, but she was someone who stood out among the people. [34] Either Miriam did not approve of Moses's wife, or she was jealous of her.

Miriam went on to question Moses's authority. She asked, "Has the Lord spoken only through Moses? Has he not spoken through us also?" (Numbers 12:2). For her words, Miriam was condemned by God and turned leprous. At Aaron's pleading, God relented but ordered that Miriam must be confined to seven days outside of the camp before she would be healed and allowed to return. At the end of the seven days, the leprosy vanished, and she was welcomed back into the camp (Numbers 12:15). After seven days, her penance was complete.

Though Miriam sinned against her bother and God, she remained loved by the people of her time and by God himself. The people loved her and refused to move to their next destination until she had been restored (Numbers 12:15). Upon her death, the wells in the desert dried (Numbers 20:2), for it was Miriam who was the keeper of the well. She was important to the survival of her people and was considered an equal of Moses and Aaron even in later centuries (Micah 6:8) and still today. Miriam was not perfect, just as we are not perfect. She made mistakes, but she repented and made atonement for her sins; and she was welcomed back into the fold, all sins forgiven and forgotten.

It is said that "Miriam's Well" appeared for centuries to those who wandered and needed encouragement to go on. The legend goes on to tell us that the well was absorbed into the Sea of Galilee, and to this day, a spring bubbles up from the depths of the lake to which devout Orthodox Jews go by boat to pray.

WE ARE MIRIAM

We all make mistakes. We all betray our loved ones in ways large and small. We all betray God. We become jealous, and we talk about others, sometimes in gossip or in spreading rumors. We often point out the flaws of others without acknowledging our own flaws. When we gain authority or power, or are close to those with authority or power, we often forsake our humility. We think we know better, or that our views are the right views, and our plans are the best plans. We begin to question those trying to help and guide us, including God.

At these times, we should pay attention to how God dealt with Miriam. We should isolate ourselves from the world, even if only for an hour. We should take the time to be alone with God, to remember who we are and to be reminded that all we do should be for the glory of God, not gain for ourselves. We need to be stricken and humbled. We need to atone for our sins. We must make a complete and sincere confession followed by penance.

Thankfully, just as with Miriam, we can confess our sins, do our penance, and be accepted back into the fold of God and his people. "The Lord is kind and merciful, slow to anger and rich in compassion" (Psalm 103:8). He wants us to

> **"The Lord is kind and merciful, slow to anger and rich in compassion" (Psalms 103).**

be with him. He forgives and forgets! He has given us the gift of the sacrament of Reconciliation so that we, too, can confess, do penance, and receive the grace of forgiveness.

The sacrament of Reconciliation is one of the many cairns the Church gives us to help us stay on our path the Heaven.

YOU ARE NOT THE SUM OF YOUR PAST SINS

Miriam sinned. She spoke against Moses and God. She questioned authority, yet she was forgiven. She is the only woman in the Bible whose childhood, adulthood, old age, death, and burial are all recorded. Her song was recorded in the Bible. She was the first prophetess and remains a beloved prophet to her people today. She is remembered primarily for her success and not for her mistakes.

Through repentance, reconciliation, and recovery, we can overcome our pasts. There is no sin so great that it can separate us from God if we truly repent.

What will separate us from the love of Christ? Will anguish, or distress, or persecution, or famine, or nakedness, or peril, or the sword? No, in all these things we conquer overwhelmingly through him who loves us. For I am convinced that neither death, nor life, nor angels, nor principalities, nor present things, nor future things, nor powers, nor height, nor depth, nor any other creature will be able to separate us from the love of God in Christ Jesus our Lord" (Romans 8:35, 37-39).

GUIDING GOD'S PEOPLE
Rahab, Deborah, and Jael

CHAPTER SIX - RAHAB

Joshua 2; Joshua 6:22-25

And Joshua the son of Nun sent two men from Shittim as spies, saying, "Go, view the land, especially Jericho," And they went and came into the house of a harlot whose name was Rahab, and lodged there. - Joshua 2:1

DELIVER US FROM EVIL

Most people are familiar with the story of the fall of Jericho and how Joshua led the men of Israel through the tumbling walls of the city. Few are familiar with the story within the story—that of Rahab the Harlot.

Joshua sent spies into the city of Jericho to "view the land" (Joshua 2:1). In other words, he wanted them to scope out the land to see what they needed to do to break through the walls and defeat the army of Jericho so they could take the city as instructed by God. News of their mission reached the king, who sent soldiers to capture and kill the spies, but a woman named Rahab took the men into her home and hid them on her roof "with the stalks of flax which she had laid in order on the roof" (Joshua 2:6). When the soldiers questioned her about the men who entered her house, she told them the men left after dark.

Figure M

Rahab was labeled as a harlot, a prostitute. Her "profession" allowed her to admit men into her house and to confess that they left "after dark." There was no questioning of her story. She was believed because of whom she was and what she did. She lied to the soldiers and saved the lives of the spies, thus allowing them to return to Joshua and tell him about the walls and the city.

Rahab was a sinner who aided God's people. God didn't need Rahab. He could have chosen someone else, someone deemed more worthy, yet God chose a prostitute to further his mission. He looked beyond her station in life and called her to participate in his plan. Despite her sinfulness, when it came down to doing what was right, Rahab helped the Israelites and gave praise to God.

God meets us where we are and offers us salvation. He assures us that his love for us is even greater than that of a mother for her child. "Can a mother forget her infant, be without tenderness for the child of her womb? Even should she forget, I will never forget you" (Isaiah 49: 15). God did not forget Rahab or the men she hid.

AIDING GOD'S PEOPLE

*But she had brought them up to the roof, and hid them
with the stalks of flax which she had laid in order on the
roof.* - Joshua 2:6

Rahab recognized that these men were sent by God, but
perhaps she recognized something more. Perhaps she
recognized that they were good men, honest men, human
beings with dignity. Perhaps her own status in life allowed
her to see them differently than others, to recognize them
as children of God.

Is Rahab's story any different from that of Mother Maria
Agnese Tribboli, who hid Jewish families in her convent in
Florence; or Caecilia Antonia Maria Loots, a school
mistress in the Netherlands who hid Jews in her small
apartment;[35] or Miep Gies who helped to hide and care for
the Frank family in Amsterdam? Like these other women,
Rahab recognized that the men's lives were worth saving
even if it meant endangering herself.

Rahab took these wanted men into her home and hid them
under stalks of flax, a plant used to make linen and held in
high regard in scripture. When Moses gave the Law, he told
the people that the high priest was to wear garments woven
with wool and linen, and linen was among the desired
offerings at the celebration of the creation of the
tabernacle. "And all women who had ability spun with their
hands, and brought what they had spun in blue and purple
and scarlet stuff and fine twined linen" (Exodus 35:25).
Linen was seen as a good and holy offering to God.
Throughout the Bible, flax and linen represent holiness and

closeness to God. The flax symbolized that God was there and was protecting them. He was present even in the house of Rahab, the Harlot.

HIDING THE JEWS FROM SOLDIERS

Maria Agnese Tribbioli was the founder of the Pie Operaie di St. Giuseppe Order and Mother Superior at the Firenze Convent in Florence, Italy. During World War II, Mother Maria took in many Jewish families, telling the other sisters that they were "homeless refugees." At one point, German soldiers tried to enter the convent but were convinced by Mother Maria to leave. When it became too dangerous for the families to stay, Mother Maria, with the help of Church clergy, aided them in their escape.[36]

Caecilia Antonia Maria Loots ran a Montessori school in Utrecht for children with severe learning disabilities. In 1942, a friend asked her to take in Jewish children to hide them from the Nazis. The devout Catholic agreed and hid them among the other children at the school. The children attended school, played around Loots's house, and took music lessons. Loots did her best to give them normal lives despite their situation. She constructed a hiding place in her attic which was used on a few occasions. In addition to the children, several adults found refuge within the school.[37]

Miep Gies hid Anne Frank and her family for twenty-five months, sacrificing her own safety to keep the Franks from the Nazis. It was Gies who discovered and saved Anne's journals which were later published as "Anne Frank: The Diary of a Young Girl."

FAITH AND WORKS

See how a person is justified by works and not by faith alone. - James 2:24

Rahab is a model of good works for both Hebrews and Christians. She reminds us that faith and works go hand in hand. In his letter to the Church, St. James asks, "What good is it, my brothers, if someone says he has faith but does not have works? Can that faith save him?" (James 2:14). Rahab exemplifies both, and James upholds her for this in the same paragraph in which he upholds Abraham for the works he did. "And in the same way, was not Rahab the harlot also justified by works when she welcomed the messengers and sent them out by a different route? For just as a body without a spirit is dead, so also faith without works is dead" (James 2:25-26).

Rahab knew and expressed three things about God. He had given the land to the Israelites; he delivered them from their captivity in Egypt; and he "is God in heaven above and on earth below" (Joshua 2:11). Rahab knew these things to be true, as did all the others in the surrounding lands and in Jericho. However, only Rahab acted on her knowledge and showed her faith through her deeds.

There is a belief by some of our Christian brothers and sisters that only faith is needed to save us. Rahab had faith. She didn't need to act upon it, but this is what God expects us to do. Rahab could have followed the law of Jericho and turned the men in or ignored their pleas for help. By putting her faith into action, she saved herself and her family. How are you putting your faith into action?

JOINING THE FAMILY OF GOD

Rahab the harlot, and her father's household, and all who belonged to her, Joshua saved alive; and she dwelt in Israel to this day, because she hid the messengers whom Joshua sent to spy out Jericho. - Joshua 6:25

When the city was ultimately taken by the Israelites, Rahab, at the instruction of the spies, hung a red cord from her window, and her mother, father, siblings, and all their children were rescued by the Israelites. Her entire family was taken under the wing of Joshua and from then on lived among the Israelites. Rahab and her family became part of a larger family—God's family.

We often judge people, not by their hearts, but by their looks; not by their souls, but by their clothing, their homes, their cars, or their professions. We do not look at people the same way Jesus does, but Rahab and Joshua did. Rahab saw the men the way Jesus would have seen them, as people worthy of being saved; and Joshua saw the same in Rahab and welcomed her into the community of the chosen people. Jesus told the chief priests, "Truly, I say to you, the tax collectors and the harlots go into the kingdom of God before you" (Matthew 21:31).

THE RED CORD

"Behold, when we come into the land, you shall bind this scarlet cord in the window through which you let us down;

and you shall gather into your house your father and mother, your brothers and sisters, all your father's household." - Joshua 2:18

For Rahab and her family to be found by Joshua, she was told to hang a red cord—a literal cairn!—from her window, thus signaling which house was hers. The red cord held great significance for the

Figure X

Israelites. It was used ceremoniously to cleanse lepers as laid out in Leviticus (Leviticus 14:6). Though we think of leprosy today as a particular disease—Hansen's Disease—in the ancient world, any kind of skin rash or abnormality was considered leprous. Thus, many of the people who were called lepers could be healed by natural means. Still, they were required to isolate, refrain from attending religious services, and announce their approach. Once healed, they had to be examined by a priest who would perform a ceremonial cleansing of the healed person. A cleansing could also be done to a house if the owner deemed it "leprous" or unclean. To perform the ceremony, "the priest shall give orders to take two live clean birds and cedar wood and a scarlet string and hyssop for the one who is to be cleansed" (Leviticus 14:4).

By hanging the red cord from her window as a means of identifying her house and its inhabitants, Rahab is declaring the house and her family as unclean. Certainly, as a harlot, she would have been seen as unclean by the people of God. She would have been ostracized in the same way that a leper would have been. Once Joshua rescued them, and they were joined to the Israelite community, Rahab and her family were cleansed, ready to begin life anew within the family of God. The red string of cleansing in Leviticus gave lepers a new life (Leviticus 14:4); the red blood on the doorposts in Exodus signaled a new life of freedom for the Israelites (Exodus 12:7); the red cord in Joshua was the gateway to a new life for Rahab (Joshua 2:18); and the blood of Jesus, which ran down his body on the cross (Isaiah 53:5) and which is given to believers in the Eucharist (Matthew 26:28), grants us all a new life through salvation.

GREAT-GREAT-GRANDMOTHER TO A KING

Rahab has been known for generations as the Harlot, but she has a much bigger and more important role for which she is remembered. Rahab, once living among the Israelites, married a man from the Tribe of Judah. Rahab and her husband, Salmon, can be found in the genealogy of Jesus as the great-great-grandparents of Israel's greatest king (Matthew 1:5). "A prostitute, she eventually becomes a legitimate wife and mother and grandmother to the greatest king of Israel: David."[38]

CHAPTER SEVEN - DEBORAH AND JAEL

Judges 4:4-22

DEBORAH - A PROPHETESS AND JUDGE

Now Deborah, a prophetess, the wife of Larridoth, was judging Israel at the time... and the sons of Israel came up to her for judgement. - Judges 4:4-5

Deborah is the only woman to have been a judge in Israel. Judges were counselors and arbiters, but also warriors and leaders. They followed in the footsteps of Moses and his successor, Joshua, prefiguring David and the kings. Deborah received a message from God that Barak, an Israelite general, was to gather warriors to fight against their oppressors, the Canaanites, who were led in battle by the general, Sisera. Barak agreed but only if Deborah would accompany him into battle. He knew he needed her intelligence and military prowess to gain victory. Deborah agreed, but told Barak, "the road on which you are going will not lead to your glory, for the Lord will sell Sisera into the hand of a woman" (Judges 4:9). Though Deborah went into battle with Barak, she took up no arms and instead "used 'weapons' of faith, humility, and acceptance of her role to win a most glorious battle."[39]

The only woman to judge the nation, Deborah was specially chosen by God, and he intended for her to be a judge and a force for good. All that she said and did came from God. Though she was the instrument of delivery, it was God's message and his will that she proclaimed and carried out. She opened herself to the will of God and judged accordingly. We can do the same if we open ourselves to the will of God and ask each day for the Holy Spirit to give us guidance and wisdom.

JAEL - A BLESSED WOMAN

Then when Barak came in pursuit of Sisera, Jael went out to meet him and said to him, "Come, I will show you the man you are looking for." So he went in with her, and there lay Sisera dead, with the tent peg through his temple. - Judges 4:22

As God promised, the Israelites prevailed in the battle, and the Canaanites fled but were struck down as they ran. Only Sisera escaped, believing he had found refuge in the tent of a woman by the name of Jael. Either Sisera did not know who had taken him in, or he was ignorant of the fact that Jael was of the tribe of Jethro, Moses's father-in-law and friend of the Israelites. After giving Sisera some milk to put him to sleep, Jael drove a tent peg through his skull, thus fulfilling the prophesy of Deborah.

Israelite Wars and the Cycle of the Four "Ds"[40]	
Disobedience	When all was good, the Israelites fell into disobedience.
Division	This caused a division between God and his people and division between the people and the rest of the world.
Defeat	Israel would be defeated by their enemies and fall back into servitude or exile.
Deliverance	They would pray to God for deliverance, and he would save them, only to have them repeat the cycle. Deborah and Jael were among the deliverers.

Once again, we see a prominent woman in the Bible singing a song of praise. Deborah's song praised Jael after the death of Sisera and victory in battle for the Israelites. Neither Deborah nor Jael accepted glory for themselves, but Deborah made sure they gave glory to God.

Most blessed of women is Jael,
the wife of Heber the Kenite,
blessed among tent-dwelling women!
He asked for water, she gave him milk,
in a princely bowl she brought him curds.
With her hand she reached for the peg,
with her right hand, the workman's hammer.
She hammered Sisera, crushed his head;
she smashed, pierced his temple.
At her feet he sank down, fell, lay still;

down at her feet he sank and fell;
where he sank down, there he fell, slain.
Judges 5:24-27

Deborah and Jael – Women Like Mary

Deborah and Jael's song contains verses similar to the beautiful Magnificat of Mary.

For he has looked upon his handmaid's lowliness;
behold, from now on will all ages call me blessed…
He has shown might with his arm,
dispersed the arrogant of mind and heart.
He has thrown down the rulers from their thrones
but lifted up the lowly…
Luke 1: 48, 51-52

Like Deborah and Rebekah before her, God spoke to Mary and told her of his plans. He instructed her in how to follow his commands. Like Jael, he used Mary to crush the enemy. Jael crushed the head of Sisera with a tent peg, and Mary's fiat crushed the head of the serpent. Once again, we see that nothing is impossible with God.

Deborah cared for the children of Israel as a mother cares for her children. She went to battle for them and for God. She and Jael assumed their roles and did what God expected of them. Then, when the battle was over, Deborah praised God for their victory. Do we lead God's children? Do we do battle for God? Do we assume the role he has given us? Do we thank him, every day, for the small and large victories to which he leads us? Are we like Deborah and Mary, accepting God's plan, working with him to achieve it, and then praising him when the plan is a success?

THE LESSONS OF DEBORAH AND JAEL

Deborah was Israel's only female judge. She was both wise and approachable. People went to her to solve their problems and end their disputes. They sought her counsel

in daily life and in battle. She used her wisdom for good. Do we seek wisdom? Do we ask the Holy Spirit to provide us counsel?

Figure O

Solomon tells us, in the beautiful book of Proverbs, "Do not forsake [wisdom], and she will keep you; love her, and she will guard you. The beginning of wisdom is this: Get wisdom" (Proverbs 4:6-7). How simple and yet profound. If we are wise, we will be guarded and protected. All we need to do is ask for wisdom. Solomon, early in his reign asked God, "Give thy servant therefore an understanding mind (wisdom) to govern thy people, that I may discern between good and evil" (1 Kings 3:9). God rewarded Solomon saying, "Behold, I give you a wise and discerning mind, so that none like you has been before you and none like you shall arise after you" (1 Kings 3:12). We must ask for wisdom, and then we must be wise enough to listen for God's voice.

Deborah heard God's voice. She spent time listening for God to speak to her, seeking him out. Just as important, when he spoke to her, she listened. She understood the needs of her people and what God wanted for them because she had an intimate relationship with him. Do we emulate Deborah? Do we take time every day to talk to God, to listen to him, and to seek his commands and desires? Are we among God's leaders?

Deborah was a woman of faith who, like Miriam, sang praise to God, "Hear, O kings; give ear, O princes; to the Lord I will sing, I will make melody to the Lord, the God of Israel" (Judges 5:3). She proclaimed God's word, praised him, and followed his commands. She led an army in a lopsided battle with little chance of winning, but she believed the word of God, and her people were victorious. Deborah knew the Lord would help her in battle for, like David, she "had success in all [her] undertakings; for the Lord was with [her]" (1 Samuel 18:14).

Deborah and Jael, both women, proved that even the least among us can do great things. If a woman could be a judge in ancient times, if a small group of people could defeat a great army, if a woman could crush the head of the enemy, the general of a great army, what more can you do if you have the wisdom and faith of Deborah and Jael? Ask God for wisdom, talk *with* God (speaking *and* listening), and know that God is with you.

BUILDING GOD'S KINGDOM
Ruth, Hannah, and Bathsheba

CHAPTER EIGHT - RUTH

Ruth 1-4

BLESSED BY THE LORD

"For where you go I will go, and where you lodge I will lodge; your people shall be my people, and your God my God; where you die I will die, and there will I be buried. May the Lord do so to me and more also if even death parts me from you." - Ruth 1:16-17

The Book of Ruth begins with the plight of Ruth and Orpah, two women of Moab, who married the sons of Elimelech and Naomi, Judeans who had settled in Moab to escape a famine in Judah. The husbands of all three women died. Naomi planned to return to her native Bethlehem and urged her daughters-in-law to return to their families. While Orpah tearfully hugged her mother-in-law and sister-in-law goodbye and returned to her family, Ruth refused to leave Naomi and accompanied her to Bethlehem. "Both Naomi and Ruth make bold decisions, reflecting the fact that widows seem to have had more independence than other women."[41] Naomi also owned land, which gave the women an advantage over many other women, married or widowed.

The two women, bold in their combined independence, become one unit, one in family and faith. Ruth "pledges her life even unto death to her. She sides with and lives in solidarity with a poor woman in a foreign country and takes on another race, another nation, another religion, and another's blood ties."[42] When Ruth chooses to stay with Naomi, Ruth claims the faith of her husband and mother-in-law for herself.[43]

Figure P

After settling in Bethlehem, Naomi sent Ruth to gather grain from the field of a relative. Ruth obediently went, following the threshers and picking up the grain that fell to the ground. She took the grain home to Naomi so they would have food. Boaz, Naomi's kin—perhaps a cousin of her husband—saw Ruth and inquired after her. When he heard she only took what had fallen on the ground and gathered the grain for food to feed herself and her mother-in-law, he became enamored by Ruth, admiring her honesty, hard work, and dedication to Naomi.

After some time, Boaz took Ruth for his wife, saying to her, "May you be blessed by the Lord, my daughter; you have made the last kindness greater than the first, in that you have not gone after young men, whether rich or old" (Ruth 3:10). Boaz and Ruth had a son, Obed, a descendant of Judah and the father of Jesse. Obed was the grandfather of Israel's great king, David, and Ruth was his great-grandmother. Ruth, a Moabite, became the grandmother of the greatest Jewish king (Matthew 1:5). God met her where she was and led her home.

A WOMAN WITH A PAST

Like Rahab, Ruth had a past. She was not a prostitute, but she was a Moabite. She was not an Israelite and not a believer in the God of Abraham. Yet she committed herself not only to her mother-in-law but to Naomi's God. When she declared that she would remain with Naomi rather than return to her family, she said, "Wherever you go I will go, wherever you lodge I will lodge; your people shall be my people and your God, my God; where you die I will die, and there will I be buried" (Ruth 1:16-17). Ruth left her past behind to go with her mother-in-law, accepting the God of Israel as her God, open to whatever God had in store for her. She did not know what her life would be like, but she had faith and trust, and God used that to fulfill his ultimate purpose. "Boaz answered her: 'All that you have done for your mother-in-law since the death of your husband has been fully told to me, and how you left your father and mother and your native land and came to a people that you did not know before. The Lord recompense you for what you have done and a full reward be given you by the Lord, the God of Israel, under whose wings you have come to take refuge'" (Ruth 2:11-12).

Ruth, again like Rahab, discovered a new life among the people of God. The Apostles and St. Paul found new life in Jesus, and St. Paul calls us to do the same. "But one thing I do: forgetting what lies behind and straining forward to what lies ahead. I press on toward the goal for the prize of the upward call of God in Christ Jesus" (Philippians 4:13-14).

A WOMAN WITH A PURPOSE

And Ruth the Moabitess said to Na'omi, "Let me go to the field, and glean among the ears of grain after him in whose sight I shall find favor." - Ruth 2:2

Ruth was given the chance to stay in Moab and return to her people. Instead, she took a giant leap of faith. She was young and might not have traveled to Bethlehem. She was raised giving praise and worship to a pagan god. She was a housewife and widow, like Naomi, with no means to support herself. Yet she trusted Naomi and Naomi's God. She let herself follow his plan and not her own. Ruth had a destiny, a purpose to fulfill. She was to become the great-grandmother of David.

We all have a purpose. We are all called to be sons and daughters of God, to take up the mission of the Apostles, and to spread the Good News. We don't always know what our mission is, the view is not always clear, the path not always marked; but we must trust in the Lord, knowing he will reveal to us our purpose as he did to Ruth. "For I know the plans I have for you, says the Lord, plans for welfare and not for evil, to give you a future and a

> For I know the plans I have for you, says the Lord, plans for welfare and not for evil, to give you a future and a hope. (Jeremiah 29:11)

hope" (Jeremiah 29:11). Ruth had faith that God would provide for her and Naomi. Through that faith, God revealed his plan.

Boaz was more than just a kinfolk of Ruth's father-in-law.

Figure Q

According to the levirate marriage custom (Deuteronomy 25:5-10), Ruth had an obligation to supply her deceased husband with an heir and was to turn to his brother after her husband's death. However, since her husband's brother was also dead, she had no way to honor her husband or his family. As a cousin of her husband, but not a brother, Boaz was not bound to marry Ruth. In fact, the story tells us that another man, perhaps closer kin, was supposed to marry Ruth, but he declined, probably because Ruth's children would have had a right to land already promised to other heirs. By offering herself to Boaz, Ruth and Boaz were both making sacrifices for the sake of her dead husband. She was giving herself to this older man whom she did not know, and he was taking on the financial burden of Ruth, Naomi, and any future children, vowing to share his estate with them. Through their sacrifice, they both discovered their purpose—to become parents and procure a legacy.

A WOMAN OF CHARACTER

*Then the women said to Na'omi, "Blessed be the Lord,
who has not left you this day without next of kin; and may
his name be renowned in Israel! He shall be to you a
restorer of life and a nourisher of your old age; for your
daughter-in-law who loves you, who is more to you than
seven sons, has borne him."* - Ruth 4:13-15

Thomas Paine, the English-American writer and political
essayist, once said, "Reputation is what men and women
think of us; character is what God and angels know of us."
Ruth had both an outstanding reputation and a remarkable
character. She was kind, loving, and a hard worker. She was
loyal to Naomi, honest in her gathering of grain, and
humble before Boaz. The people knew all that she had
done for Naomi and how hard she labored to provide their
food. She was given the highest of praise by the other
women when they described her to Naomi as "your
daughter-in-law who loves you, who is more to you than
seven sons" (Ruth 4:15).

Just as the people knew and admired Ruth's reputation,
surely God and the angels knew of her character. Ruth was
a woman of abiding loyalty and devotion who, through
faith, found great joy. She found a home, love, redemption,
and prosperity because she was faithful and obedient. Ruth
came from nothing. She was a woman of no material worth
raised in a pagan land, but she had character, and God met
her where she was and molded her into a woman of
prominence, a woman of faith, "a woman of worth" (Ruth

3:11). She left behind a legacy that brought us a king, for it was through her great-grandson, David, born of her marriage to Boaz, that we received Jesus, a true testament to the regard in which God and his angels held her.

Pray that you will find the trust in God that Ruth found. Pray for humility. Pray that your work will be for the good and will be pleasing to those around you and to the Lord. Care for your parents and your spouse's parents. Welcome children from God. Be like Ruth, a woman of character, a true cairn along our path to Heaven.

CHAPTER NINE - HANNAH

1 Samuel 1; 2:1-11; 21

POURING OUT HER SOUL BEFORE THE LORD

"I am an unhappy woman. I have had neither wine nor liquor; I was only pouring out my heart to the LORD."
- 1 Samuel 1:15

Hannah was married to Elkinah who had two wives, Hannah and Peninnah. While Peninnah was able to give Elkinah many children, Hannah was unable to conceive. Peninnah taunted and ridiculed Hannah mercilessly and would "provoke her sorely, to irritate her, because the Lord had closed her womb" (1 Samuel 1:5). Year after year, Hannah would put up with these provocations, never complaining or letting on to anyone that she was in anguish. Hannah prayed fervently to the Lord to look upon her with pity and grant her a child, whom she would dedicate to the Lord. "As soon as the child is weaned, I will bring him, that he may appear in the presence of the Lord, and abide there forever" (1 Samuel 1:22).

Hannah visited the tabernacle and prayed, not with her mouth but with her heart. "She speaks to God, not with noisy requests, but in the silence of her heart, for she knows that the Lord hears the heart rather than the voice. And she receives what she asks for because she asks with faith" (St. Cyprian, On the Lord's Prayer 5). [44] Though Hannah felt pain and distress because of her husband's other wife, she did not insult Peninnah nor wish the other woman harm. Instead, Hannah prayed for her own condition to change, for God to "look on the affliction of your maidservant" (1 Samuel 1:11).

Hannah prayed so fervently and with such passion, Eli the priest thought she was drunk. He told her to put away her wine and go home, but Hannah told him she had "been speaking out of my great anxiety and vexation" (1 Samuel 1:16), to which Eli responded that God would grant her prayer.

This is what God wants from us. He wants us to be passionate in prayer. He wants us to go to him with our requests because he wants to give us whatever our hearts desire, as long as our desires are good and pleasing to him. Jesus told his disciples, "Ask and it will be given to you; seek and you will find; knock and the door will be opened to you. For everyone who asks, receives; and the one who seeks, finds; and to the one who knocks, the door will be opened" (Matthew 7:7-8).

God does not want us to talk about or insult others, harbor anger, or suffer alone. He wants us to bring our worries, resentments, and fears to him. God tells us, "Come to me, all you who labor and are burdened, and I will give you rest. Take my yoke upon you and learn from me, for I am meek and humble of heart; and you will find rest for yourselves. For my yoke is easy, and my burden light" (Matthew 11:28-30). God wants us to ask him; he wants to hear from us and wants to grant our requests, share in our grief, and help carry our burdens. He wants us to ask for and strive for change within ourselves, not wish that others would become more like we wish them to be.

GIVING BACK TO THE LORD WHAT IS HIS

Year after year, Hannah prayed for a son, and God answered her prayer. It was not in her time, but in his time that Hannah conceived a child and was true to her word.

Figure R

As soon as Samuel was weaned, she took him to the tabernacle, saying to Eli, "For this child I prayed; and the Lord has granted me my petition which I made to him. Therefore I have lent him to the Lord; as long as he lives, he is lent to the Lord" (1 Samuel 1:27). The name Samuel means *the name of God* or *one who is from God*. Samuel was God's gift to Hannah in return for her prayerful request, just as Hannah's dedication of the son was her grateful return of that gift back to the Lord.[45]

Can you imagine? Here is the child Hannah so desperately wanted, the child she begged God to give her, the child she carried and bore and nursed; and she took him to Eli and left him there to be raised by the priests as a child of God. Hannah gave up her child for God, and she was blessed with a son like no other. "Now the boy Samuel continued to grow both in stature and in favor with the Lord and with men" (1 Samuel 2:26).

Think of the women who give up their children for adoption when they know this is what's best for the child. How difficult this must be for many of them. Like Hannah, they know what is best for their children and how to give their child the future they deserve. Sometimes this involves allowing someone else to raise the child even when the decision to do so is a painful one. These are the times when giving back the child to God means giving the child to someone else and trusting that God will take care of the rest.

I have a good friend who has four boys. I remember when her youngest was born, she said to us, "I pray that one of these boys becomes a priest someday." My husband marveled at this, surprised that she would give up her child willingly to the Church, but she was insistent that to have a child become a priest would be a gift. I think of my friend when I think of Hannah. She knew her sons were gifts from God, and she knew she had to return those gifts in some way. Inspired by the Holy Spirit, Hannah gave back to God what was already his, and Samuel was called to serve the Lord.

Our children, our homes, our livelihoods, everything we have within our possession are all gifts from God. We have nothing of our own accord. Even those things we have earned, we earned through the talents and wisdom God has granted us. "Naked I came from my mother's womb, and naked I shall return; the Lord gave, and the Lord has taken away; blessed be the name of the Lord" (Job 1:21).

> **"The Lord gave, and the Lord has taken away; blessed be the name of the Lord." (Job 1:21)**

PROMISES KEPT WITH JOY

By giving Samuel back to God, Hannah kept the promise she made when she prayed for a child. God expects us to keep our promises to each other and most importantly to him. "Do not swear, either by heaven or by earth or by any other oath, but let your 'yes' be yes and your 'no' be no, so that you may not fall under condemnation" (James 5:12). Hannah was a woman of her word, one who kept her promises, and we need to do the same. We should always strive to let our "yes" be yes and our "no" be no, not only to God but to others.

Hannah not only kept her promise, she did so with joy. She left her son with Eli, the priest, and inspired by the Holy Spirit, prayed a song of rejoicing, adoration, encouragement, and prophesy. How blessed she was by the Lord in her suffering, and how beautifully she exclaimed her blessings.

My heart exults in the Lord, my horn is exalted by my God. I have swallowed up my enemies; I rejoice in your victory.

There is no Holy One like the Lord; there is no Rock like our God.

Speak boastfully no longer, do not let arrogance issue from your mouths. For an all-knowing God is the Lord, a God who weighs actions.

The bows of the mighty are broken, while the tottering gird on strength.

The well-fed hire themselves out for bread, while the hungry no longer have to toil. The barren wife bears seven sons, while the mother of many languishes.

The Lord puts to death and gives life, casts down to Sheol and brings up again.

The Lord makes poor and makes rich, humbles, and also exalts.

He raises the needy from the dust; from the ash heap lifts up the poor, to seat them with nobles

and make a glorious throne their heritage. For the pillars of the earth are the Lord's, and he has set the world upon them.

He guards the footsteps of his faithful ones, but the wicked shall perish in the darkness; for not by strength does one prevail.

The Lord's foes shall be shattered; the Most High in heaven thunders; the Lord judges the ends of the earth. May he give strength to his king, and exalt the horn of his anointed!

1 Samuel 2:1-10

Again, the woman's song foreshadows Mary's Magnificat (Luke 1:46-56). Mary received the gift of a son from the Father. She raised Jesus and taught him the ways of their people. She loved him and stood by his side until his death when she gave her son back to the Father.

Hannah found joy in being able to bring a son into the world. She was no longer barren, and after Samuel, she had many other children with Elkinah. She came to fully understand what St. Paul later explained to the Romans, "We even boast of our afflictions, knowing that affliction produces endurance, and endurance, proven character, and proven character, hope, and hope does not disappoint, because the love of God has been poured out into our hearts

> **Affliction produces endurance, and endurance, proven character, and proven character, hope, and hope does not disappoint (Romans 5:1-5).**

through the Holy Spirit that has been given to us" (Romans 5:1-5). When confronted with pain and suffering, we must not lose hope, for having hope allows us to persevere, and perseverance brings joy.

It's hard to imagine Hannah's pain when she left the priest's tent without her son, but think of the joy in her heart when she thought of her son being raised as a man of God. It's even harder to imagine Mary's pain as she stood at the foot of the cross, but think of her joy on Easter Sunday when she looked upon her son who was raised from the dead by God. When we suffer and persevere, and when we give back to God that which he has given to us, we are greatly rewarded with unfathomable joy.

CHAPTER TEN - BATHSHEBA

BATHSHEBA, THE SURVIVOR
2 Samuel 11; 12:15-25; 1 Kings 1:28-31; 2:13-25

From the roof he saw a woman bathing; she was very beautiful. David sent people to inquire about the woman and was told, "She is Bathsheba, daughter of Eliam, and wife of Uriah the Hittite, Joab's armor-bearer." - 2 Samuel 11:2-3

Figure 5

King David was a man after God's own heart...until he wasn't. Upon seeing Uriah's wife, Bathsheba, David's mind focused only on her and not on God. He told his servants to bring the married woman to him, and he "took her" and "lay with her" (2 Samuel 11:4). We don't know if Bathsheba went to the palace willingly, if she went because she was ordered by the king, or if she slept with David of her own accord. What we do know is that she became pregnant, and when David's plans failed to trick Uriah into thinking the child was his, David had Uriah killed. Thus began the relationship of King David and Bathsheba.

We must assume that Bathsheba did not go willingly with David. When Uriah was killed, Bathsheba mourned for him, making "lamentation for her husband" (2 Samuel 11:27). When her mourning ended, David sent for her, and she became his wife. We don't know if she ever learned that it was David who caused the death of Uriah nor whether she came to love David once she was married to him, but we know that she had little choice either way. To refuse the king would have been a death sentence. She was a victim of David's lust and then a victim of David's power and authority.

Many women have walked in Bathsheba's shoes and have, perhaps, learned from her example, not as a victim but as a survivor. Every day, she had to live with, sleep with, and bow down before her aggressor, but she had her son, and later she had the promise from God that her son would be the next king. How difficult it must have been for Bathsheba to live the life she'd been handed. How often she must have lamented about her plight, but she had faith that God would use her suffering for good "We know that all things work for good for those who love God, who are called according to his purpose." (Romans 8:28). God doesn't make bad things happen, nor does he condone atrocities such as rape or abuse, but he can use these terrible actions for a greater good. In time, through Solomon, Bathsheba became the most powerful woman in Israel. "She was a survivor, a reminder to all who experience sexual assault that they are

> "We know that all things work for good for those who love God, who are called according to his purpose" (Romans 8:28).

not alone, that God sees them in their suffering, that he is still working in their lives."[46]

We don't know how Bathsheba felt once she was the Queen Mother. Did David's regret and repentance, expressed so humbly in the Psalms, extend to her? Did she spend her life missing her first husband? Did she grow to love David? Did she find comfort in the success of her son? These are questions to which the scriptures give us no answers. What we do know is that Bathsheba chose to go on, to survive—for survival is a decision, one that requires trust in God and love of self. "Bathsheba's decision to survive...made her a reminder to all of us that God can bring glory out of even the messiest of lives."[47]

How do we decide to go on? There's only one way to proceed when we are faced with the most difficult decisions or events in life—we must pray. In those challenging times, ask the Holy Spirit for guidance. Stay close to the Lord and let him comfort you. Perhaps David wrote these words upon observing all the pain he had inflicted on his wife, "The Lord is close to the brokenhearted and saves those who are crushed in spirit" (Psalm 34:18).

THE MOURNING MOTHER

David comforted his wife, Bathsheba, and went in to her, and lay with her. - 2 Samuel 12:24

Bathsheba bore a son, but as foretold by the prophet
Nathan, the child was sick and died. David prayed to the
Lord for forgiveness, recognizing he had turned his back
on God and needed to repent. He wept for his child and
for himself. The only mention of Bathsheba during this
time of mourning for her son is that "David comforted his
wife...and lay with her; and she bore a son, and he called
his name Solomon" (2 Samuel 12:24). God granted her a
second child, but certainly, this did not take away from the
pain of losing her first son. No mother would need to be
told more about how Bathsheba felt than those few words,
"David comforted his wife."

Here is a woman who may have been taken against her will,
learned she was pregnant, lost her husband in battle, and
was brought to marry the king as soon as her mourning
ended. It may have been that the only bright spot in her life
was the child growing within her womb. Like many other
women, Bathsheba brought a child into this world who was
not meant to remain here. Though the Bible does not detail
how she responded to her child's death, all women possess
the knowledge of how she felt and know how she grieved.
Bathsheba's name could be substituted for Rachel's in the
words spoken by God to Jeremiah, "A voice is heard in
Ramah, lamentation and bitter weeping. Rachel is weeping
for her children; she refuses to be comforted" (Jeremiah
31:15). The name of any woman who has lost a child or
someone she thought of as a child could be used; it would
be almost impossible for her to be comforted.

Bathsheba did find comfort in time, not just from David but in the birth of many other children, including Solomon. Her grief, turned to joy, foreshadowed Mary's. Like Mary, Bathsheba gave life, mourned the death of her child, and yet believed in the hope and promise of life again.[48] She lost her first child but rejoiced at the birth of Solomon. Mary saw Jesus crucified but was present when he revealed himself after the resurrection.

THE QUEEN MOTHER

"Make your request, my mother; for I will not refuse you."
- 1 Kings 2:20

Though it seems that Bathsheba's second pregnancy happened immediately upon the death of their newborn, we don't have a chronology that tells us exactly how old the first child was when he died, how long Bathsheba was in mourning, or when the couple next conceived. We do know that Bathsheba eventually bore Solomon. Before the death of David, Solomon was declared king by his father. Bathsheba then had a crucial role to fill—that of the Queen Mother.

When we think of the Queen Mother today, we probably think of the mother of Queen Elizabeth II, a noble woman who was once queen but relinquished her queenship once her daughter ascended to the throne. In the ancient world, this was not the case. The wife of the king was not the queen; she was merely the king's wife, typically one of many wives and concubines to provide him with heirs. How could there be one queen, with all the royal power the title conveys, when a king had multiple wives and even more mothers of his children? This problem was solved by declaring the mother of the king as queen. In fact, the Hebrew word for queen, *gebirah*, was only used in scripture to refer to the mother of a king.

It was not the king's wife but his mother who sat on the throne beside him, advised him, and took petitions to him. Jeremiah referred to rulers as "the king and the queen mother" (Jeremiah 13:18). It was the queen mother who had the king's ear and his confidence, not to mention his loyalty. "The queen

Figure T

mother was not merely treated with deference by the monarch, but…she held a significant official political position superseded only by that of the king himself."[49]

When Bathsheba approached Solomon with a petition, his response was, "Make your request, my mother; for I will not refuse you" (1 Kings 2:20).

> **"Make your request, my mother; for I will not refuse you" (1 Kings 2:20).**

Bathsheba's role had changed from that of wife and supplier of an heir to a "counsellor and a source of wisdom." [50] It is believed that the queen mother "functioned as a counsellor in the political and judiciary affairs at court and perhaps as a mediator."[51] She had power and authority and, though not an equal to the king, was respected, revered, and sought after as an intercessor and mediator. Bathsheba was an intercessor between Solomon and his people just as Mary is our meditator with Jesus.

INTERCESSOR OR MEDDLER?

So Bathsheba went to King Solomon to speak to him…And the king rose to meet her and bowed down to her…Then she said, "I have one small request to make of you; do not refuse me." And the king said to her, "Make your request, my mother, for I will not refuse you."
- 1 Kings 2:19-20

There is an argument that can and has been made that Bathsheba was not a mediator but an opportunist, thus rendering Mary's position as Jesus's mother meaningless. As seen with many of the Biblical patriarchs and rulers, including Abraham's son and Issacs's son, the older sibling was often passed over as the heir. This was the case with Adonijah, son of David and Haggith (2 Samuel 3:4)—next in line after the deaths of his older brothers—and David and Bathsheba's son, Solomon. As the elder brother, Adonijah felt it was his birthright to become the next king. Unfortunately for Adonijah, God chose Solomon to assume the throne. "Of all my sons (the Lord has given me many sons) he has chosen Solomon my son to sit upon the throne of the kingdom of the Lord over Israel. He said to me: 'It is Solomon your son who shall build my house and my courts, for I have chosen him to be my son, and I will be his father'" (1 Chronicles 28:5-6).

When David was on his deathbed, being nursed by his concubine, Abishag, Adonijah declared himself king. All his other brothers, the leader of the army, and the chief priest supported him. Bathsheba, recalling the Lord's vow to David, told her husband about Adonijah's actions so that before his death, David decreed that Solomon was the new king. After his father's death, Adonijah went to Bathsheba and asked her

Figure U

to intercede on his behalf and ask Solomon to give Abishag to him as a wife. In those days, when a son slept with his father's concubine, he was considered the new king (2 Samuel 16:21-22). The request was a way for Adonijah to become king through the back door, so to speak. Bathsheba took the request to Solomon, who told her he would not refuse her, but was so angered by his brother's appeal that he ordered Adonijah to be killed. How can we see the queen mother as an intercessor if her son promises to give her what she asks and then kills the recipient of her request?

Let us consider that Bathsheba knew what was going on here. Certainly, as a citizen of Jerusalem as well as the wife of King David, she knew the traditions of the region. Why would she, after going through the trouble of making sure her son was decreed to be the king, usurp his power by helping his brother steal the throne? On the contrary, she kept her promise by taking Adonijah's appeal to Solomon and relaying the request diplomatically, knowing that her son was going to deal with his brother in his own way.

When we go to Mary, we can be assured that Mary hears us and that she goes to her son on our behalf, but what if our request is not in our best interest or goes against God's plan for us? In that case, wouldn't God assure his mother that he will listen and grant her request but then upon hearing it, explain to her that his answer may not be what we had hoped it would be? How often are we told that God always listens but only gives us what he feels is best or what we need rather than what we want? How often do mothers implore their husbands on their children's behalf only to learn that the request cannot be granted for reasons unknown or misunderstood by the child? St. James explained that we often pray for the wrong things, focusing not on our needs but on our wants. "You do not have, because you do not ask. You ask and do not receive, because you ask wrongly, to spend it on your passions" (James 4:3).

> **You ask and do not receive, because you ask wrongly, to spend it on your passions (James 4:3).**

The Catechism of the Catholic Church says, "Do not be troubled if you do not immediately receive from God what you ask him; for he desires to do something even greater for you, while you cling to him in prayer. God wills that our desire should be exercised in prayer, that we may be able to receive what he is prepared to give."[52] Often, what we ask for is not what we need or what is right as was the case with Adonijah. Sometimes, we need to prayerfully discern what it is we should be asking for or prayerfully ascertain why a prayer was not granted (or granted in the way that it was). In either case, the key is to continue to pray so that we may understand how and why God grants our prayers. As with Adonijah, there are times when the answer to our request is just the opposite of that for which we prayed, and we must be prepared for that answer.

Bathsheba was not trying to cause trouble between David's sons nor was she trying to trick Solomon. She did as she promised and took the appeal to her son. From there, it was up to her son to decide how to handle the request. David, Solomon's father and the author of the Psalms, understood that we sometimes ask for things out of malice or jealousy or greed. He prayed, "If I regard wickedness in my heart, the Lord will not hear" (Psalm 66:18).

The Lord, who knows our hearts, will know if our requests are done for the right reasons and if they are in accordance with his will. We may not always like the answer we receive from the Lord, but the answer will always be what is best.

PROTECTING GOD'S KINGDOM
Judith and Esther

CHAPTER ELEVEN - JUDITH

Judith 8-13: 14:1-10; 16

BLESSED BY THE MOST HIGH

She was beautiful in appearance, and had a very lovely
face; and her husband Manas'seh had left her gold and
silver, and men and women slaves, and cattle, and fields;
and she maintained this estate. No one spoke ill of her,
for she feared God with great devotion. - Judith 8:7-8

A strange yet familiar tale is told in the Book of Judith,
echoing the virtues of Rachel and Ruth and the victories of
Deborah and Jael while foreshadowing the words spoken
of Mary. The tale is not part of the Jewish canon and never
has been but appeared in the Septuagint, the first Greek
translation of the Old Testament. It exists in ancient
Hebrew writings. It is seen as Biblical literary fiction but
has been proclaimed canonical by several Roman Catholic
councils (Rome, Hippo, Carthage, Florence, and Trent)
because of its important allegory.[53] The Greek Orthodox
Church also includes Judith in its canon.[*] The name Judith

---

[*] To be part of the Church's canon is to be included in the
catalogue of inspired writings known as the Old and New

literally means, "Jewish woman," so the implication is clear that Judith stands in for Israel in her story.

According to scripture, Judith (representing Israel) lived during the reign of the Babylonian king, Nebuchadnezzar, though none of the events told within the book took place during his kingship, and the Nebuchadnezzar of the story was said to be king of Syria, not Babylon. Many scholars believe that the king in the original telling of Judith was not named; thus, a Greek translator substituted the name Nebuchadnezzar as he would have been widely known as a king who reigned in the region. Whatever the name might have been, the king sent his general, Holofernes (who represents all the invaders and enemies of Israel), to lead an army that would mow down all the neighboring lands, including Israel.

Judith was a very devout woman who "lived at home as a widow for three years and four months. She...wore the garments of her widowhood...she was prudent of heart, discerning in judgment, and quite virtuous" (Judith 8:4-7). Like the tribes of Israel, she followed the Law. Upon hearing of the distress of the elders about the forthcoming battle, Judith devised a plan to save her people. She did not share her plan but asked the elders to give her three days to carry it out.

Testaments, identified as such by the Church. The Book of Judith is included in the Roman Catholic Canon as truth and not literature.

Judith gave up her fast, removed her mourning clothes, "bathed her body with water and anointed herself with precious ointment, and combed her hair and put on a tiara, and arrayed herself in her most festive apparel" (Judith 10:3). She went into the camp of Holofernes and seduced him. Rather than impugn her chastity, she got him drunk on a "great quantity of wine" (Judith 12:20) so that he would pass out, and she beheaded him. Upon her return to Israel, with the general's head in the sack of her maidservant, Judith was hailed as "blessed by the Most High God above all women on earth" (Judith 13:18).

Figure 1

Though Judith's story is fictional, it is a cairn which contains many points that we should adhere to. Like Rachel and Ruth, Judith possessed beauty, poise, and confidence. Leaders listened to her, and men's hearts were "ravished with her" (Judith 12:16). Like Deborah, Judith was a leader who made plans, dictated them, and carried them out. She knew how to get people to listen to her and do what she told them to do. She was like Woman Wisdom in Proverbs, who called over the city, "Let whoever is naive turn in here; to any who lack sense I say, Come, eat of my food, and drink of the wine I have mixed! Forsake foolishness that you may live; advance in the way of understanding" (Proverbs 9:4-6). She used her beauty to lure the foolish general to his death. Judith was a woman who we should all try to emulate.

A WOMAN OF WORDS

"Who are you that have put God to the test this day, and are setting yourselves up in the place of God among the songs of men? You are putting the Lord Almighty to the test."- Judith 8:12-13

Judith was unafraid to point out to the men that they were wrong. She warned them that they were testing God and making promises in his name that went against God's own wishes. She accused them of pretending to read God's mind, warning that they were going to provoke his anger.

Most of the women of the Old Testament had very little to say. Other than Deborah the Judge, most are quoted with a line here or there and often a song, but rarely an entire discourse. Judith voiced two such discourses, one to Uzziah the elder and a second to Holofernes and his army. Throughout the book named for her, Judith gave many orders and false words of praise and exhortations while carrying out her plan. She was not afraid to speak and not afraid to tell others what needed to be done. Most importantly, she pointed out that Uzziah and the elders were taking on the role of God and putting God to the test.

Women often shy away from speaking up and speaking out. For centuries, women have been treated as the inferior sex whose ideas are silly or frivolous. The writers of the scriptures understood and acknowledged the wisdom of women like Deborah and Judith. When they spoke, people listened. When they planned, people agreed. When they acted, their deeds were rewarded. Their successes could be found in their knowledge of when to speak and what to say. Again, Woman Wisdom teaches us all we need to know: "Do not reprove the arrogant, lest they hate you; reprove the wise, and they will love you. Instruct the wise, and they become still wiser; teach the just, and they advance in learning" (Proverbs 9:8-9).

In addition to Proverbs, we have another source for helping us speak words of wisdom. We should always rely on the Holy Spirit and ask him to fill our mouths with the right words. "When they bring you before the synagogues and the rulers and the authorities, do not be anxious about

> **"The Holy Spirit will teach you in that very hour what you ought to say" (Luke 12:12).**

how or what you are to answer or what you are to say, for the Holy Spirit will teach you in that very hour what you ought to say" (Luke 12:12). "And when they bring you up, do not be anxious beforehand about what you are to say; but say whatever is given you in that hour, for it is not you who speak, but the Holy Spirit" (Mark 13:11). Like Judith, who prayed before each of her discourses and before her night with Holofernes, pray before you speak and before you act. Ask the Holy Spirit to put words in your mouth and guide your actions so you are speaking and doing the work of God. Remember to let God be God, and man or woman be man or woman. We are not to put God to the test. We are to pray for guidance from the Holy Spirit and to "do whatever he tells you" (John 2:5).

A WOMAN WHO WORKED FOR JUSTICE

O Lord God of all might, look in this hour upon the work of my hands for the exaltation of Jerusalem. For now is the time to help your inheritance, and to carry out my undertaking for the destruction of the enemies who have risen up against us. - Judith 13:4-5

Holofernes was not an honorable or righteous man, to say the least. He was working his way across the Mid-East, taking down everyone and everything in his path. Judith knew that there was only one way to stop a man like that. Of course, we see her actions as being just as barbarian as his, but times were different back then. There were no international accords, no courts at the Hague, and no way to mete out justice other than through violence or oppression. Judith did what she had to do to stop the man's reign of terror and save her people.

If we stop and look at her story piece by piece, though, we see that all Judith's actions were reenactments of past heroes of Israel. She is another example of the woman crushing the head of the enemy (Genesis 3:15). Judith is blessed by the high priest as Abram was by Melchizedek (Genesis 14:19-20). She models the actions of Jael with the blow of the general's head (Judges 4:17-24) and repeats the actions of David severing the head of Goliath (1 Samuel 17:51). Her story is a retelling of the people of Israel and what their heroes did for the good of the nation.

Today, we have many ways to work for justice for the good of our people. We can do volunteer work, participate in a walk or protest, or lobby our political leaders. We must follow the words of the prophet, Micah, "what does the Lord require of you but to do justice, and to love kindness, and to walk humbly with your God" (Micah 6:8). We must

> **To do justice, and to love kindness, and to walk humbly with your God (Micah 6:8).**

also follow Paul's decree to the Romans, "Beloved, never avenge yourselves, but leave it to the wrath of God; for it is written, 'Vengeance is mine, I will repay,' says the Lord" (Romans 12:19). For it is not enough to seek justice. We also must show mercy and leave vengeance to God.

THE WOMAN STRIKES THE HEAD OF THE ENEMY

O daughter you are blessed by the Most High God, above all women on earth; and blessed be the Lord God, who created the heavens and the earth, who has guided you to strike the head of the leader of our enemies. - Judith 13:18

"I will put enmity between you and the woman, and between your seed and her seed; he shall bruise your head, and you shall bruise his heel" (Genesis 3:15). These were the words spoken to the serpent in the Garden of Eden. After Judith returned to Israel, Uzziah praised her and echoed the words of God in saying, "O daughter you are blessed by the Most High God, above all women on earth;

and blessed be the Lord God, who created the heavens and the earth, who has guided you to strike the head of the leader of our enemies" (Judith 13:18). Another woman would come many years later whose offspring would strike at—bruise—the head of the enemy.

The story of Judith is a foreshadowing of what was to come. An enemy has come to strike down all people as he makes his way toward God's chosen ones. He takes no prisoners, preferring to end lives and gather souls in his quest for greatness and his goal to rule over all the earth. The new Eve, who comes after Judith, will be told, in almost the same exact words, "Blessed are you among women, and blessed is the fruit of your womb" (Luke 1:42). Her offspring will conquer the enemy. Our Protestant and Jewish brothers and sisters may question whether Judith existed and if she was the one who conquered the enemy, but we can be assured that the woman Judith foreshadowed, Mary, did live and did give birth to Jesus, the one who conquered Satan through his death and resurrection.

CHAPTER TWELVE - ESTHER

Esther 11; 12; 1; 2; 3:1-13;13:1-7; 3:14; 4; 13:8-18;
14; 5:1-2; 15; 5:3-14; 6-7; 8:1-12; 16; 8:13-16;9-11*

GUARDIAN OF HER PEOPLE

The king loved Esther more than all the women, and she
found grace and favor in his sight more than all the virgins,
so that he set the royal crown on her head and made her
queen. - Esther 12:17

The book of Esther is one of only three books in the Bible
named for a woman and one of the few books that does
not take place in Israel or among the Israelites. It reads like
a fairy tale, a story that easily could be the plot of a Disney
movie. It tells of a young orphan's rise from lowliness to
power, from peasant to queen, from an unknown Jewish
girl to a woman heralded by her people for all generations.

A young orphan, raised by her uncle in the land of Persia,
Esther is a Jewish girl with little hope of advancing in the

---

* The disarrangement of chapter and verse order in the Book of
Esther is due to the insertion of the deuterocanonical portions in
their logical place in the story, as narrated in the Greek version
from which they are taken. In the Latin translation by St. Jerome,
these passages were placed after the story.

world. Her uncle, Mordecai, saves King Ahasuerus of Persia by uncovering and foiling an assassination attempt on his life. Because of this, though he does not know the name of the person who saved him, King Ahasuerus looks kindly on the Jews; however, others in his court do not. When his chief counsellor, Haman, accuses the Jews of treason, it is Esther who cleverly intervenes to prevent the annihilation of her people.

CHOSEN FOR A REASON

"Who knows whether you have not come to the kingdom for such a time as this." - Esther 4:14

King Ahasuerus is in search of a new queen after deposing his wife and banishing her from the palace for disrespecting him and his royal position. At her uncle's urging, Esther joins the other virgins from throughout the land in a year-long "beautification" process to learn how to be a queen and properly assume the royal duties. However, she never reveals to anyone in the court that she is Jewish. The king, loving Esther above all the others for her poise and beauty, takes her for his wife without knowing she is Mordecai's niece and of Jewish descent. The young, self-conscious girl becomes the Queen of Persia.

At the urging of his chief counsellor, Haman, the king is convinced to wage genocide against all Jews living in Persia. Haman is angered that Mordecai follows the God of Israel and does not bow to the king or his court; thus, Haman vows "to destroy all the Jews, the people of Mordecai, throughout the whole kingdom" (Esther 3:6). Mordecai hears of the plan and sends word to Esther, charging her "to go to the king to make supplication to him and entreat him for her people" (Esther 4:8).

At first, Esther refuses, fearing the king will enact retribution on her for daring to enter the inner court without being summoned and for asking the king to listen to her. Mordecai's reply is, "Think not that in the king's palace you will escape any more than all the other Jews...and who knows whether you have not come to the kingdom for such a time as this" (Esther 4:13-14).

Figure W

Who knows whether you have not come to the kingdom for such a time as this? Have you ever wondered about coincidence versus providence? Were you meant to be in a certain place at a certain time, or to meet a particular person or witness a specific event? We all play a role in God's plan. We all have our mission within his mission. There is no such thing as coincidence. Rather, when we find ourselves in just the right place at just the right time, or with that particular person, or witnessing that event, we are there because God put us there. We were meant to be there, to discover a cairn, and to be an instrument in the musical masterpiece God is composing. True, we might not save a nation, but we may never know the far-reaching implications and impacts that our words and actions have on others. Like Seurat's pointillist painting, we all seemingly are random dots that are connected to create a beautiful picture only God can discern from his place in Heaven. We all have a purpose to fulfill in the mission of God. "Let each person lead the life that the Lord has assigned to him, and to which God has called him" (1 Corinthians 7:17).

> Let each person lead the life that the Lord has assigned to him, and to which God has called him. 1 Corinthians 7:17

THE POWER OF PRAYER

And Esther the queen, seized with deathly anxiety, fled to the Lord…And she lay upon the earth together with all her maidservants, from morning until evening…On the third day, when she ended her prayer, she took off the garments in which she had worshipped and clothed herself in splendid attire. - Esther 14: 1,3; 15:1

Esther did not want to approach the king. She was afraid and unsure of herself, filled with "deathly anxiety," but "fear can accompany faith without replacing it."[54] After three days of prayer and fasting, she changed her mind and organized a banquet at which she exposed Haman and his plan to destroy her people. Esther spoke to the king, telling him she was Mordecai's niece, and falling "at his feet and besought him with tears to avert the evil design of Haman the Agagite and the plot which he devised against the Jews" (Esther 8:3). Esther was afraid, but prayer and fasting gave her the power to follow the counsel of Psalms, "Cast your burden on the Lord, and he will sustain you; he will never permit the righteous to be moved" (Psalms 55:22). Because she prayed for help and was righteous in her actions and supplications, God was with her. "Prayer is the best

> **"Prayer is the best weapon we possess. It is the key that opens the heart of God." - Padre Pio**

weapon we possess. It is the key that opens the heart of God" (Padre Pio).

Through the power of prayer and help from God, Esther found the courage and fortitude to approach the king and reveal the actions of Haman and to beg her husband to save the Jewish people of Persia. She humbled herself before the king, falling at his feet, and was sincere in her plea for help. She did exactly what St. Peter advises us to do. "Humble yourselves therefore under the mighty hand of God, so that he may exalt you in due time. Cast all your anxiety on him, because he cares for you" (1 Peter 5:6-7). "Our strength is prayer, and the prayer of a humble person is the weakness of God. The Lord is weak only in one sense: He is weak before the prayers of his people."[55] This does not mean that God is weak but that he is moved to pity and wants to help us when we pray. Like a father who cannot resist the humble pleas of his daughter, like the king who cannot resist the humble pleas of Esther, God cannot resist our humble pleas and prayers.

As God exalts us when we approach him with humility, King Ahasuerus exalted Esther, for it was not just out of love for his wife, but because of the respect that Esther showed to him that her wishes were granted and expanded upon. The king proclaimed all enemies of the Jewish people were to be destroyed, and he and Esther declared a festival to be celebrated every year to commemorate the events that took place thanks to Esther's pleas.

> **Purim is celebrated on the 14th or 15th day of the month of Adar, usually in March. It is always one month before Passover and begins with the Fast of Esther. The primary directive of the holiday is to hear the reading of the Book of Esther. The verses of "redemption" (Esther 2:5; 8:15–16; and 10:3) are read in a louder voice than the other verses. It is traditional to boo, hiss, stomp feet, and shake noisemakers each time the name of Haman is mentioned in the service. The people are encouraged to feast and drink as much wine as they can during the festival which is a day of friendship and celebration of the work God does through others.**

Most of us will never bow before a king, and most of us will never plead on behalf of a nation or intervene to stop its destruction; however, we all do things throughout our lives that make a difference in the lives of others. Like Esther, we need to pray for strength and guidance. We need to ask the Holy Spirit to help us discern our path, and we need to praise the Lord when all is said and done.

PART II
WOMEN OF THE NEW TESTAMENT

MOTHERING THE NEW KINGDOM
Mary and Elizabeth

CHAPTER THIRTEEN - MARY

Luke 1:26-56; 2; John 2:1-12; John 19:17-30

WHOLEHEARTEDLY, YES

"Blessed are you among women, and blessed is the fruit of your womb!" - Luke 1:42

Imagine yourself a young Jewish girl, around the age of fourteen, recently betrothed[*] to a man from your village. Your entire life is laid out before you—marriage, a family, a quiet life in the small, inconsequential town of Nazareth, the anticipation of grandchildren, growing old with your husband, and living humbly until the hour of your death. Your heart is full of dreams and promises of a stable future. Then one day, out of the blue, something happens to you that you've heard about but has only happened to the

---

[*] In those days, marriage was a two-step process for Jewish couples. Mary may or may not have known Joseph prior to their betrothal (*erusin*). These were deals made by the father of the bride and were typically done without consultation of the young woman. Betrothal was the first step in the process. The couple was legally married, but the woman would still live with her parents until the actual wedding (*nissuin*), sometimes for as long as a year or two. The couple would not consummate their marriage until their actual wedding night.

prophets and their wives, something you've heard in the
Torah and Talmud
and marveled at with
your classmates. An
angel of the Lord
appears to you to
share with you God's
plan. Like Rebekah
and Deborah before

Figure X

you, God has brought you into his knowledge. Eve
hungered for this knowledge, but it was to a lowly young
girl that God began to unravel the mystery of his plan
through the words of an angel.

What does this mean? Fear and awe overcome you as the
angel hails you, "full of grace." A sense of peace settles as

> "You have found favor with God. And behold, you will conceive in your womb and bear a son" (Luke 1:28, 30-31).

he assures, "Do not be
afraid." Your heart beats
faster at the words, "you
have found favor with
God. And behold, you will conceive in your womb and
bear a son" (Luke 1:28, 30-31). Can your mind register
what he says next? How can you possibly grasp the
meaning of "Son of the Most High," "the throne of his
father David," or "of his kingdom there will be no end"
(Luke 1:32-33)? You are shocked further by the news that
your cousin, Elizabeth, a woman of advanced age, is also
with child by the decree of God.

How would you respond to this? How could you possibly understand all the angel has conveyed? Can you imagine bowing humbly before the angel and saying, "Behold, I am the handmaid of the Lord; let it be done to me according to your word" (Luke 1:38)?

> "Behold, I am the handmaid of the Lord; let it be done to me according to your word" (Luke 1:38).

The Catechism states,

> Thus, giving her consent to God's word, Mary becomes the mother of Jesus. Espousing the divine will for salvation wholeheartedly, without a single sin to restrain her, she gave herself entirely to the person and to the work of her Son; she did so in order to serve the mystery of redemption with him and dependent on him, by God's grace.[56]

Figure Y

To put it simply, without hesitation, without fearing for her life or her future, without doubting the angel's words, but with her whole heart, Mary said yes. She said yes to God, to Jesus, and to the world. "Her deep humility and readiness to say yes to the Lord are revealed in the fact that faced with God's superabundance, she doesn't ask 'Why?' but rather, 'How?'"[57]

"The Father of mercies willed that the Incarnation should be preceded by assent on the part of the predestined mother, so that just as a woman had a share in the coming of death, so also should a woman contribute to the coming of life."[58] Justin Martyr wrote,

> For Eve…having conceived the word of the serpent, brought forth disobedience and death. But the Virgin Mary received faith and joy when the angel Gabriel announced the good tidings to her that the Spirit of the Lord would come upon her, and the power of the Highest would overshadow her; wherefore the Holy Thing begotten of her is the Son of God.[59]

Eve conceived the "word of the serpent" while Mary conceived the "Word of God."[60]

Over and over, throughout scriptures, God tells us not to be afraid. We are counselled to put our trust in the Lord. The prophets reveal God's message as, "Do not fear, for I am with you, do not be afraid, for I am your God; I will strengthen you, I will help you, I will uphold you with my victorious right hand" (Isaiah 41:10). Yet we falter; we question. We back away and say, not I, not that. We feel unable or unworthy, even when faced with the smallest tasks. We say no; but Mary, a young, betrothed girl, said yes to the greatest feat that has ever taken place on earth.

Like Esther, in assuming her role in God's mission, Mary assumed her role. Esther, Queen of Persia, set the example for Mary, Queen of Heaven. She prayed, discerned, and looked to God for answers and guidance; and though she was filled with deathly anxiety, she accepted God's call to save his people. Imitating Esther, Mary trusted in God and accepted his call to bear Jesus, pondering all his words, thus saving all mankind. St. Irenaeus said, "The knot of Eve's disobedience was loosed by the obedience of Mary."[61]

THE ULTIMATE WOMAN OF GOD

"Let it be done to me according to your word." - Luke 1:38

Think about the women who went before her, the ones Mary would have learned about as a young woman, ones she would have known from the Torah. Mary's mother would have used their stories to teach Mary about faith, courage, and trust in God. The Catechism tells us,

> Throughout the Old Covenant the mission of many holy women prepared for that of Mary. At the very beginning there was Eve; despite her disobedience, she receives the promise of a posterity that will be victorious over the evil one, as well as the promise that she will be the mother of all the living. By virtue of this promise, Sarah conceives a son in spite of her old age. Against all human expectation God chooses those who were considered powerless and weak to show forth his faithfulness to his promises: Hannah, the mother

of Samuel; Deborah; Ruth; Judith and Esther; and many other women. Mary "stands out among the poor and humble of the Lord, who confidently hope for and receive salvation from him. After a long period of waiting the times are fulfilled in her, the exalted Daughter of Sion, and the new plan of salvation is established."[62]

We have seen that all the women of the Old Testament were precursors of Mary. Their words, actions, and faithfulness were small and fleeting compared to Mary's. Eve was the first Mother of Creation, and Sarah was the Mother of Nations. Rebekah aided God in his plan for his people; and Deborah was a nurse, teacher, and caregiver like Mary, who nursed, taught, and cared for Jesus. Rachel mourns for the children of Israel, and Mary mourns for all God's children when we go astray. Rachel and Leah told Jacob "whatever God has said to you, do" (Genesis 31:16); Mary told the wine stewards at Cana, "Do whatever he tells you" (John 2:5).

Deborah and Jael were models for their people, and Mary is a model for all people. Hannah sang of God's praises in a song that is echoed by Mary's Magnificat, and Judith crushed the head of her enemy as Mary's offspring will crush the head of Satan. Bathsheba gave us a clear understanding of Mary's role as the Queen Mother, and Esther rose to assume her place in God's mission, just as Mary did with her fiat. Though all these women shared a part in God's story of salvation and acted as cairns for

Mary's journey, Mary played the biggest role of them all. To her, "God entrusted such tasks as feeding his son with her own milk, singing him to sleep, and accompanying him all the way to the cross, where she gave her sorrowful yes to his self-offering."[63] Jesus's entire human life depended upon the yes of Mary.

Mary spoke only four times in all the New Testament, but each time, she taught us a valuable lesson. She showed what it means to trust completely in God, "let it be done to me according to your word" (Luke 1:38). She went at once to help her cousin in need and upon arrival, like the women before her, she sang God's praises, "but Mary makes their words and her own refer not to the past but to the future."[64]

> My soul proclaims the greatness of the Lord; my spirit rejoices in God my savior.
> For he has looked upon his handmaid's lowliness; behold, from now on will all ages call me blessed.
> The Mighty One has done great things for me, and holy is his name.
> His mercy is from age to age to those who fear him.
> He has shown might with his arm, dispersed the arrogant of mind and heart.
> He has thrown down the rulers from their thrones but lifted up the lowly.
> The hungry he has filled with good things; the rich he has sent away empty.
> He has helped Israel his servant, remembering his mercy, according to his promise to our fathers, to Abraham and to his descendants forever (Luke 1:46-56).

Upon finding Jesus in the temple, Mary said, "Behold, your father and I have been looking for you anxiously" (Luke 2:48), but when he asked, "Did you not know that I would be in my Father's house?" (Luke 2:49), Mary did not answer. Instead, she "kept all these things in her heart" until that day in Cana when she was the one who told Jesus that indeed, his hour had come.

A WOMAN OF STRENGTH

"Do whatever he tells you." - John 2:5

"O, woman, what have you to do with me? My hour has not yet come" (John 2:4) were the words that Jesus spoke to his mother when she asked him to help their friends who had run out of wine. We can picture the scene: Mary and Jesus are attending the wedding of good friends—so good that Jesus is allowed to bring his disciples,

Figure 7

and Mary is let in on the family's shameful secret that the wine has run out—when Mary approaches her son for help. Jesus gently takes his mother by the arm and leads her into a corner, away from the crowd. He looks intently into her eyes, speaking soul to soul, and tells her that his hour has not yet come. *Do you know what this will mean?* his expression reads. *Do you understand what will come next?* his mind says to hers.

Mary's mind races back to the words of the angel, to Jesus's birth and the strange visits from shepherds and kings, to the presentation when Simeon told her, "Behold, this child is set for the fall and rising of many in Israel, and for a sign that is spoken against (and a sword shall pierce through your own soul also)" (Luke 2:34-35), and to the day when Jesus said that he was in his father's house. She recalls their many conversations around the dinner table, the times she read to him from the Torah, and he explained to her what the words meant and how they pointed to him, and how he made her brush her fingers along the wood he worked with and laid the nails in her hand, describing what God had planned for him. With all these things that she kept in her heart and pondered for thirty years, Mary nods and gives the command that will set their undeterrable course as Mother and Son. She has chosen the road they will travel, and after this day, their lives will never be the same.

It was at Cana where Mary once again interceded for her people. She began her role as intercessor with her yes to the angel, for who speaks for and to a baby but the mother? She continued that role when she counseled Jesus to help with the wine, but she deferred to him in saying, "Do whatever he tells you" (John 2:5). Like Bathsheba who interceded for Adonijah, Mary interceded for the bride and groom.

For the next three years, the mother, Mary, followed the child, Jesus. She was with him when he preached, when he revealed to the world who he is, when he celebrated the Last Supper, when he was scourged and mocked and made to carry his cross, and when he breathed his last breath. "Standing by the cross of Jesus were his mother, and his mother's sister, Mary the wife of Clopas, and Mary Magdalene" (John 19:25). It was into Mary's arms that the crucified Christ was laid, and from her arms that Joseph of Arimathea took his lifeless body to lay it in the tomb. St. Bernardine said, "All the sorrows of the world united would not be equal to the sorrow of the glorious Mary."

"Thus the Blessed Virgin advanced in her pilgrimage of faith, and faithfully persevered in her union with her Son unto the cross. There she stood, in keeping with the divine plan, enduring with her only begotten Son the intensity of his suffering, joining herself with his sacrifice in her mother's heart, and lovingly consenting to the immolation of this victim, born of her." [65] Pope Francis said, Mary "never lost her peace of heart, a

> Mary "never lost her peace of heart, a fruit of having abandoned herself with trust to the mercy of God."
> - Pope Francis

fruit of having abandoned herself with trust to the mercy of God." [66] It has been said that, even at the foot of the cross, Mary never lost faith and knew Jesus would rise again. It was her belief in the Resurrection that got her through the crucifixion. We can believe, as Saint John Paul the Great did, "that Jesus showed himself first to his

Mother, who had been the most faithful and had kept her faith intact when put to the test."[67]

From conception and labor to the foot of the cross, Mary walked by her son's side and shouldered his burdens as her own, moving forward with the faith that her son was the Lord and would return to her as promised. In her we see "the preeminent way in which she embodies the perfect life of the believer."[68] Who better than she for us to call upon to help carry our burdens and lead us in faith?

THE MODEL DISCIPLE

"And his mother kept all these things in her heart." - Luke 2:51

Mary has been called the first Christian and the model disciple. Pope Francis said, "Mary, the first and most perfect disciple of Jesus, the first and most perfect believer, the model of the pilgrim Church, is the one who opens the way to the Church's motherhood and constantly sustains her maternal mission to all mankind."[69] Jesus himself told us how exalted Mary is when a woman in the crowd said to him, "Blessed is the womb that bore you," and Jesus answered, "Blessed rather are those who hear the word and keep it" (Luke 11:27-28). Was Jesus telling us that his mother was not blessed? No! He was telling us the reason she is blessed is not because she carried Jesus in her womb but because she heard his word, the word of his father, and kept it. She kept it in the way she answered the angel, and she kept it as she pondered all these things in her heart.

According to St. Augustine, "She kept truth safe in her mind even better than she kept flesh safe in her womb. Christ is truth, Christ is flesh; Christ as truth was in Mary's mind, Christ as flesh in Mary's womb; that which is in the mind is greater than what is carried in the womb."[70]

I heard once that the first Beatitude was not spoken at the Sermon on the Mount but at the visitation of Mary to Elizabeth. After John the Baptist leaps in his mother's womb, Elizabeth says, "And blessed is she who believed that there would be fulfillment of what was spoken to her from the Lord" (Luke 1:45). Blessed is she

Figure AA

who believed. Blessed is Mary, the first to recognize that Christ was the Son of God, the first to say yes to God's call to follow his Son, and the first example of how we are to act as Christians—by believing in the fulfillment of what was spoken by God—that Jesus Christ is our Redeemer.

Saint John Paul the Great said that Mary's fiat was just the beginning of her walk as a Christian. Her yes was "the point of departure from which her whole 'journey towards God' begins, her whole pilgrimage of faith."[71] Her trust in God allowed her to say yes, and it sustained her through all the sorrows she endured. Mary's example, that of the first and model Christian, should be the one we strive to follow—

to say yes to God, trust in him completely, do his will, allow his will to rule our lives, and never turn away from Christ even during the darkest moments. Most importantly, when God calls, we need to answer with haste. Just after the Annunciation, Mary "arose and went with haste into the hill country of Judah, and she entered the house of Zechariah and greeted Elizabeth" (Luke 1:39-40). "For centuries Israel had heard the words of Yahweh, but more often than not the people were sluggish in responding. The true Israelite, once she had heard the word of the Lord, moved!"[72]

BEHOLD THY MOTHER

When Jesus saw his mother, and the disciple whom he loved standing nearby, he said to his mother,, 'Woman, behold your son!' Then he said to the disciple, 'Behold your mother!' And from that hour, the disciple took her to his own home. - John 19:26-27

At the Council of Ephesus in 431AD, a great debate ensued over the notion of Mary being the mother of God. Pope Celestine I, with support from St. Cyril of Alexandria, reiterated to the Council "that a mother does not give birth to a nature; she gives birth to a person."[73] The council fathers taught that Jesus was not just a person with an intense relationship to God, *or* God in Heaven, *or* man on earth. On the contrary, they upheld the four-hundred-year teaching that Jesus *is* God, echoing St Irenaeus, a follower of John the Apostle and Evangelist in the first and second centuries. "And this meant, they concluded…if Jesus was divine and Mary was the mother of Jesus, then Mary could and should be called the Mother of God." [74] At the announcement of the decision, the people of Ephesus paraded through the streets in a joyful, torch-lit parade, glorifying the Mother of God.

As the Israelites had a mediator in The Queen Mother, Bathsheba, we are blessed to have a mediator in the form of a queen mother ourselves. We have the mother of our King—the Blessed Virgin Mary. In an address to the people in St. Peter's Square in 1954, Pope Pius XII said,

> In Holy Writ, concerning the Son whom Mary will conceive, We read this sentence: 'He shall be called the Son of the most High, and the Lord God shall give unto him the throne of David his father, and he shall reign in the house of Jacob forever, and of his kingdom there will be no end,' and in addition Mary is called 'Mother of the Lord'; from this it is easily concluded that she is a Queen since she bore a son who, at the very moment of His conception . . . was also as man King and Lord of all things. [75]

In the passage the Pope quoted from Luke 1:32-33, Mary is the mother of Jesus, the Son of the Most High, the heir to the throne of his father David, the one who will reign forever, whose kingdom will have no end. If Jesus is this King of whom the angel spoke, then clearly, Mary is the Queen Mother. St Ambrose told us, "She is mother of the

Church, for she brought forth him who is the Head of the Church."[76]

In the words of St. Elizabeth, Mary is "the mother of my Lord" (Luke 1:43). If, according to St. Elizabeth, the Council of Ephesus, and Pope Pius XII, Mary is Jesus's and God's mother, and Jesus is our brother, doesn't that make Mary our mother, too? What evidence is there to support this? The supreme evidence—the words of Jesus. With his dying breath, Jesus gave us his mother as our own.

The Apostle John, in his Gospel, is representative of us. Throughout his recounting of the life of Jesus, John was writing not just as an Apostle and disciple[*] of Jesus but also, like Mary, as an example of the quintessential Christian. "The Beloved Disciple" is John in the Gospel, but he is meant to be us. John wrote all of us into his Gospel and called us "Beloved"; therefore, when Jesus speaks to John in his Gospel, he is also speaking to us. At the foot of the cross, "Jesus saw his mother, and the disciple whom he loved standing nearby, he said to his mother, 'Woman, behold your son!' Then he said to the disciple, 'Behold your mother!' And from that hour, the disciple took her to his own home"

> **Then he said to the disciple, 'Behold your mother!' And from that hour, the disciple took her to his own home"** (John 19:26-27).

---

[*] Apostle vs disciple – Jesus chose twelve Apostles who, aside from Judas Iscariot who was replaced by Matthias, were the first Pope and Bishops of the Church. Those who closely followed Jesus throughout his ministry, including but not limited to the Apostles, were his disciples.

(John 19:26-27). We are expected to take our mother, Mary, into our homes and love her like our earthly mothers.

By declaring that Mary is John's mother, Jesus also declared her to be our mother. In one sense, Jesus was looking out for the welfare of his beloved mother. In another, he was looking out for the welfare of his beloved followers. St. John Vianney said, "Jesus Christ, after having given us all he could give, that is to say, the merit of his toils, his sufferings, and his bitter death; after having given us his adorable body and blood to be the food of our souls, willed also to give us the most precious thing he had left, which was his holy mother." Mary is our mother and the Mother of the Church, the mother of all of those who profess the faith. Bishop Barron wrote,

> If Mary is the one through whom Christ was born, and if the Church is indeed Christ's Mystical Body, then she must be, in a very real sense, the Mother of the Church. She is the one through whom Jesus continues to be born in the hearts of those who believe. This is not to confuse her with the Savior, but it is to insist on her mission as mediator and intercessor.[77]

CHAPTER FOURTEEN - ELIZABETH

Luke 1:5-25, 39-66

RIGHTEOUS AND BLAMELESS

And when Elizabeth heard the greeting of Mary, the child leaped in her womb; and Elizabeth was filled with the Holy Spirit. - Luke 1:41

In contrast to what we have read about other childless women in the Bible, we do not read anywhere that Elizabeth was angry or desperate or praying to bear children. Nowhere is this behavior of the other women chastised or looked down upon, but there is profound meaning in Elizabeth's barren state. She accepted her role in God's plan as a childless woman. Even after the words of the angel came to pass, and she found herself with child, "for five months she hid herself saying, 'Thus the Lord has done to me in the days when he looked on me, to take away my reproach among men'" (Luke 1:24-25). It was not Elizabeth who looked down upon herself for being barren but the others within their circle.

What a great blessing it is to accept not being able to have children and see it as a part of God's plan. Though Elizabeth did eventually conceive, she lived most of her life without having children, "righteous before God, walking in all the commandments and ordinances of the Lord blamelessly" (Luke 1:6). Luke is pointing out that Elizabeth was not barren because she sinned, as was the belief in those days. She was, in fact, righteous and blameless; she accepted the decrees of the Lord and his will. Elizabeth and Zechariah were both "advanced in age," and it is clear from the text that, until this time, Zechariah had no children. Unlike the patriarchs, he did not have other wives or concubines. Theirs was a marriage distinct and holy—they were devoted to God and each other. They had no children because it was part of God's plan. Their day, when they would become parents, was to come in God's time and in God's way, and they would be blessed beyond measure. Zachariah and Elizabeth can be seen as the first Christian couple, living the Good News according to the teachings of the New Covenant rather than the ways of their ancestors.

PREPARING FOR THE COMING OF THE LORD

"Prepare the way of the Lord, make his paths straight."
- Isaiah 40:1-11; Mark 1:1-8

When the angel foretold the birth of John the Baptist, he said, "he will go before him in the spirit of Elijah, to turn the hearts of the fathers to the children, and the disobedient to the wisdom of the just, to make ready for the Lord a people prepared" (Luke 1:17). John was to prepare the world for Jesus. Like her son, Elizabeth had an important job to do in preparing someone for the coming of the Lord. In her sixth month, Elizabeth was able to help Mary understand the changes her body would go through, and Mary was able to witness Elizabeth's last three months of pregnancy.

Elizabeth was the first to outwardly recognize Mary as the mother of God, alerted to the fact by her son, John. "And why is this granted to me that the mother of my Lord should come to me? For behold, when the voice of your greeting came to my ears, the child in my womb leaped for joy" (Luke 1:43-44). Elizabeth proclaimed the first beatitude, "And blessed is she who believed that there would be a fulfillment of what was spoken to her from the Lord" (Luke 1:45). Elizabeth was the

> **"And blessed is she who believed that there would be a fulfillment of what was spoken to her from the Lord" (Luke 1:45).**

first to know of Mary's pregnancy, the one who helped her through morning sickness, and the one who counseled her on what to tell her parents and her betrothed. She would have advised her younger cousin on how to answer their questions and how to live with the scorn. After all, Elizabeth the barren had endured a lifetime of scorn until she became pregnant with John. For three months, the women cried together, laughed together, and prayed together. Elizabeth helped guide Mary on her journey.

We are meant to be Elizabeth to other women. We are meant to hold their hands, counsel them, advise them, teach them, laugh and cry with them, and pray with and for them. We are meant to lead them to the Lord and prepare them to accept him lovingly and without trepidation.

It is believed that Elizabeth had already passed before the beheading of her son, but surely Mary felt her cousin's pain. She cried at the loss of the babe who leaped with joy, the child she helped to deliver, and the realization that she, too, would suffer much the same loss. Even in death, Elizabeth was preparing Mary for what was to come when Mary would witness the death of her own child. Like Elizabeth, we are charged with the task of helping prepare other women for their role in God's mission.

Figure BB

THE BIRTH OF CHRISTIANITY

And the child grew and became strong in spirit, and he was in the wilderness till the day of his manifestation to Israel. - Luke 1:80

There is some debate about Mary's presence at the birth of Elizabeth's son, John. St. Ambrose, Byzantine Archbishop Theophylactus, and the venerable St. Bede all contended that Mary was there to help her cousin with the birth as did Archbishop Fulton Sheen. "Mary is present at three births: at the birth of John the Baptist, at the birth of her own Divine Son, and at the 'birth' of John the Evangelist, at the foot of the Cross, as the Master saluted him: 'Behold thy mother!'"[78]

It matters not whether Mary was at the birth. What matters is that Elizabeth's child, who leaped for joy at the coming of Mary and the baby in her womb, recognized who Mary was and so did his mother. From conception to death, he preached about Jesus. He was a humble man, saying, "He must increase, but I must decrease" (John 3:30) and "As for me, I baptize you with water; but One is coming who is mightier than I, and I am not fit to untie the thong of his sandals; He will baptize you with the Holy Spirit and fire" (Luke 3:16). Surely, John learned his humility from his mother, the woman who said, "And why is this granted me that the mother of my Lord should come to me?" (Luke 1:43).

Elizabeth accepted her condition without complaint. She honored her husband and God with her compliance and steadfastness. She accepted a child in her old age as a true gift, not something she deserved or begged for. She welcomed Mary into her home and sheltered her, showing her what was to come. And with her words of humility, she set the example for her son to follow. From the moment she heard Mary's greeting, Elizabeth knew that she and her son were the humble foreshadowing of Mary and Jesus.

"Blessed are the poor in spirit, for theirs is the kingdom of heaven" (Matthew 5:3). Blessed are those who are humble, for to be poor in spirit is to be rich in faith. It is indicative of a person whose humility allows him or her to grasp our fundamental reliance on God.[79] When we rely on God and not on ourselves or others, we display the greatest form of humility. Both Elizabeth and John the Baptist knew this. He spent his entire adult life in the desert, living by God's word and God's hand alone. He "wore a garment of camel's hair, and a leather belt around his waist; and his food was locusts and wild honey" (Matthew 3:4). He recognized Jesus, not just in the womb, but by the Jordan and proclaimed, "Behold, the Lamb of God who takes away the sins of the world" (John 1:29).

Elizabeth taught her son well. She was humble and relied on God. If these are the only things we teach our children, we will have done God justice. Elizabeth is a true role model for Christians. Her child was the first evangelist, and she taught him "to do justice, and to love kindness, and to walk humbly with God" (Micah 6:8). With the birth of John the Baptist, the one who went before Jesus "to make straight the way of the Lord" (John 1:23), we have the birth of Christianity. Elizabeth's child was raised by a mother who is to be emulated by all Christian women.

GATHERING THE NEW KINGDOM
Peter's Wife, The Canaanite Woman,
The Hemorrhaging Woman, and
Photina, The Samaritan Woman

CHAPTER FIFTEEN - PETER'S WIFE

Luke 4:38-41; 1 Corinthians 9:3-5

A MYSTERY YET UNSOLVED

And he...entered Simon's house. Now Simon's mother-in-law was ill with a high fever, and they asked him about her. And he stood over her and rebuked the fever, and it left her; and immediately she rose and served them. - Luke 4:38

There is much debate among Catholic theologians, and among scholars of other faiths, about the existence of Peter's wife. Clement of Alexandria, one of the early Church Fathers, wrote in his Stromata—a history of the early Church—of Peter and his wife in Rome. "The blessed Peter, on seeing his wife led to death, rejoiced on account of her call and conveyance home,

Figure CC

and called very encouragingly and comfortingly, addressing her by name, 'Remember thou the Lord.' Such was the marriage of the blessed and their perfect disposition towards those dearest to them." [80] According to St. Clement, Peter's wife was martyred just before the Apostle himself was martyred.

Other theologians and scholars contend that Peter was a widow at the time of his Apostleship because only his mother-in-law is mentioned in the Gospels. "And he [Jesus] arose and left the synagogue, and entered Simon's house. Now Simon's mother-in-law was ill with a high fever, and they asked him about her. And he stood over her and rebuked the fever, and it left her; and immediately she rose and served them" (Luke 4:38). However, let's note the wording of the passage, "they asked him about her." Who is this "they" who asked? Perhaps it was Peter and his brother, Andrew. Mark's account of the story says that house belonged to Peter and Andrew, but Matthew's account says the house belonged to Peter. Either way, the house was Peter's and his family's dwelling. Perhaps it was Peter and his wife who asked Jesus about Peter's mother-in-law. What loving daughter wouldn't reach out to the Lord asking him to heal her mother?

We do have another clue about Peter's wife, one from St. Paul. In his letter to the Corinthians, he asked, "Don't we have the right to be accompanied by a wife, as the other apostles and…Cephas?" (1 Corinthians 9:5). According to Paul, Peter's wife was among the disciples, accompanying them on their mission.

Between Paul's words to the Corinthians and St. Clement's eyewitness account, we can assume that Peter's wife was alive when Peter was called to follow the Lord. Furthermore, it appears she did not pass while Peter was with Jesus but that she was alive until she preceded him in death in Rome. Not since the writings of St. Clement confirmed her to be alive has there been anything discovered to dispute that she alive and well and supportive of her husband's ministry. Supportive she must have been to have suffered martyrdom, remembering the Lord, before the eyes of her husband.

Let us then, based on the writing of St. Paul, go with the supposition that Peter's wife was alive when he was called to be an Apostle. Let us believe that she supported her husband and proclaimed the Gospels alongside him until her death. If this was the case, and I see no reason to believe otherwise, then she was a woman of deep understanding and great patience, a woman of faith, and a loyal and loving wife.

AN UNDERSTANDING AND PATIENT WOMAN

"Truly, I say to you, there is no man who has left house or wife or brothers or parents or children for the sake of the kingdom of God, who will not receive manifold more in this time, and in the age to come eternal life." - Luke 18:28-29

Though some Biblical works of fiction and media representations of Peter portray him as a poor fisherman, this most likely was not the case. Peter owned his own boat. He had men who worked for him. He invited Jesus to live in his house with his family. More likely, Peter was a man of means. He could support a business and a family. His mother-in-law lived with the family in a "multigenerational household," which was not customary in the first century.[81] Where was Peter's wife during this time?

Peter himself gives us a clue when he asks "Behold, we have left our homes and followed you" to which Jesus said, "Truly, I say to you, there is no man who has left house or wife or brothers or parents or children for the sake of the kingdom of God, who will not receive manifold more in this time, and in the age to come eternal life" (Luke 18:28-29).

Does this passage mean that Peter abandoned or divorced his wife? Jesus told the Pharisees, "Have you not read that he who made them from the beginning made them male and female, and said, 'For this reason a man shall leave his father and mother and be joined to his wife, and the two shall become one'? So they are no longer two but one. What therefore God has joined together, let no man put asunder" (Matthew 19:4-7). Why would Jesus have gone against his own teaching and forced Peter to leave his wife?

It's more likely that Peter's wife, understanding the important mission her husband had undertaken, stayed home to care for her mother and the rest of their family.

Furthermore, "what appears to be opposition to Christian women as public leaders (1 Cor 11:10) may have involved debate over the propriety of women appearing in the public square."[82] Women were expected to be at home, but women like Peter's wife broke this mold as they proclaimed the Good News.[83] They set an example for us, cairns along our journey.

The role of women was based on Psalm 45, "All glorious is the princess within, with robes interwoven with gold" (Psalm 45:13). This was interpreted to mean that the realm of the wife was in her home. "The way of a woman is to sit in her home, and the way of a man is to

Figure DD

go out to the marketplace and learn understanding from others."[84] It would not have been unusual for Peter to go out on his mission, to "learn understanding" from the Lord, while his wife stayed home.

I can easily empathize with Peter's wife. For the first twenty-six years of my marriage, my husband, Ken, was rarely home. His job kept him away for long hours, sometimes days at a time; and eventually, he went to work for a global company based in Rome and traveled extensively for three or four weeks of the month. I did most of the housework and raising of our children. I worked full time for the first half of our marriage, until I was able to stay home with our girls.

Did Peter's wife lie in bed at night, alone and longing for her husband? Did she curse this mission of his, praying that he would return to their family and the life she was used to? Did they argue about what was best for their marriage and their family?

Though we don't know the answers to those questions, we do know—according to St. Paul and St. Clement—that Peter's wife was a disciple herself which means she had a good understanding of the importance of his mission. She went with him to Rome and, perhaps, on his other travels. She gave her life for the Lord, remembering him as she walked to her death. As our girls grew older, I began traveling more with my husband. I'm sure the same was true of Peter's wife. Until such time, though, all the domestic work would have fallen on her in Peter's absence.

How often do we find ourselves in the place of Peter's wife? With few exceptions, aren't wives usually the ones to stay at home, or even if they work, the ones who manage the household? Much has been made about the fact that Peter's wife was not with him throughout his time with Jesus, but wasn't she? If not in body, then in spirit? When one's spouse is away, aren't the thoughts of the spouse at home with the one who is gone? Aren't the love and the longing there? It's so easy for us, with computers and phones, to stay in touch when we or our spouse are away from our homes and families. Imagine how hard it must have been for Peter's wife not to know where her husband was, to fear he might be in danger, to wonder when or *if* he was coming home? We often say one has the patience of Job, but what about the patience of the wife of Peter?

And what of those who are not wives or mothers? We assume Peter had a family, but we don't know this as fact. Perhaps his wife was childless and taking on a different, but just as important, role. Society would have dictated it was her place, her mission even, to stay in Capharnaum and stoke the home fires, taking care of her ill mother so Peter could fulfill his mission. There are many women who choose to stay home or take a back seat so others may rise and lead, not out of selfishness but out of selflessness.

Many married and unmarried women alike recognize their role to take care of those around them—mothers and fathers, siblings, friends, elderly neighbors, and other members of their community—so others can take up the call to lead. This, in no way, means those women are not following God's call. They are just acting more discreetly, perhaps recognizing the words of John the Baptist, "He must increase; I must decrease" (John 3:30). For others to rise to their full potential, it may be necessary for people in their lives to quietly tend to needs in the background.

OBEDIENT UNTO DEATH

A man shall leave his father and mother and be joined to his wife, and the two shall become one flesh. - Genesis 2:24

There is much said about the following scripture reading:

> Be subject to one another out of reverence for Christ. Wives, be subject to your husbands, as to the Lord. For the husband is head of the wife as Christ is head of the Church, his body, and is himself its Savior. As the Church is subject to Christ, so let wives also be subject in everything to their husbands. Husbands, love your wives, as Christ loved the Church and gave himself up for her, that he might sanctify her, having cleansed her by the washing of the water with the word. Even so, husbands should love their wives as their own bodies. He who loves his wife loves himself. For no man ever hates his own flesh, but nourishes and cherishes it, as Christ does the Church, because we are members of his Body. "For this reason a man shall leave his father and mother and be joined to his wife, and the two shall become one flesh." This is a great mystery, and I mean in reference to Christ and the Church; however, let each one of you love his wife as himself, and let the wife see that she respects her husband (Ephesians 5:21-33).

Many modern-day women eschew this passage, seeing it as old-fashioned and demeaning. To believe this is to misunderstand the passage and its beauty. What St. Paul is telling us is that, like Christ who died for his Church, a husband must be willing to die for his wife. His love must be so strong, so true, and so pure, that he will lay down his life for her. In return, the wife should respect and honor her husband. Through the Holy Spirit, man and woman, as one flesh, love each other through mutual respect. "The Spirit which the Lord pours forth gives a new heart, and renders man and woman capable of loving one another as Christ has loved us."[85]

> "The Spirit which the Lord pours forth gives a new heart, and renders man and woman capable of loving one another as Christ has loved us" (Saint John Paul the Great).

"In his wife he [man] sees the fulfillment of God's intention: 'It is not good that the man should be alone, I will make him a helper fit for him,' and he makes his own the cry of Adam, the first husband: 'This at last is bone of my bones and flesh of my flesh'" (Genesis 2:18, 23).[86] As a husband, a man fulfills his humanly intention as decreed by God, but he and his wife must see themselves as fulfilling God's plan for each of them through one another. Paul says, "Be subject to one another out of reverence for Christ." The love, respect, and support for each other must be mutual. A woman cannot respect a man who is not willing to do everything in his power to take care of her, and a man cannot be willing to die for someone who does not show him respect and honor. Husbands are called to die for their wives! This is figurative, of course, as a husband must die to himself, to his personal needs, and to his worldly desires; but it is literal as well. Christ literally died for his bride, the Church.

The man is the head of the family as Christ is the head of the Church which means that a husband must submit himself wholly to Christ to be a good husband. This is not about status. It is about making sure both the husband and the wife reach Heaven. Pope Paul VI's *Gaudium et Spes* tells us "Authentic married love is caught up into divine love…so that this love may lead the spouses to God."[87]

Moreover, the passage is about holding each other accountable to God. It's about being subject to one another in reverence for Christ and about recognizing the dignity of each other. "The family finds in love the source and the constant impetus for welcoming, respecting and promoting each one of its members in his or her lofty dignity as a person, that is, as a living image of God." [88]

Peter's wife stayed home to take care of their family while Peter accepted his role as Christ's follower, student, missionary, and eventually, head of the Church. We are all asked to fill a role in our missionary purpose. Perhaps in your family, the wife goes to work while her husband stays home and manages the household. This is not contrary to St. Paul's teaching. It is perfectly aligned with it! As long as there is mutual respect, support, love, and a true recognition of dignity between a husband and a wife, they are fulfilling their roles in life and in the Church. "Above all it is important to underline the equal dignity and responsibility of women with men."[89] Saint John Paul the Great referred to this as "spousal complementarity."

Peter's wife had a primary role which was to care for her family, a role which was just as important as Peter's role in the Church. No matter how we live our lives, women are called to take care of their families. "The true advancement of women requires that clear recognition be given to the value of their maternal and family role."[90] Likewise, an unmarried woman, or a woman without children, may be called upon to tend the needs of her parents, her siblings, or her neighbors. Those without children have been given the gift of performing "other important services to the life of the human person, for example...various forms of educational work, and assistance to other families and to poor or handicapped children."[91]

Of course, the daily care of children, aging parents, or even one's community does not last forever. Just as I did when my children were older and my husband was away, Peter's wife saw her role change, and she joined him on his missionary travels. This understanding is required of us as followers of Christ. Married women are to work together with our spouses to teach our children about God; to set an example of a holy, Christian home and family; and then to take the Good News to the world. "Among the fundamental tasks of the Christian family is its ecclesial task: the family is placed at the service of the building up of the Kingdom of God in history by participating in the life and mission of the Church."[92]

Peter's wife accepted her role in the family as well as her role in the spreading of the Gospels, and she accepted her death. Like Jesus died for the Church, St. Peter and his wife also died for the Church. Together until the end, even when apart, they followed the teachings of Christ and lived holy lives. With the knowledge learned at the feet of Christ, St. Peter brought his wife into the Church, and together, they spread the word until their deaths.

We are given the same charge. Married or not, we are to live our lives for Christ first and then for those others within our care. We are to carry his word to the rest of the world where we may face persecution and even death. We must die to ourselves and sanctify each other, cleansing each other through the Word. Like Peter and his wife, may all men and women, at the hour of death, rejoice on account of our call and conveyance home, and call encouragingly and comfortingly, 'Remember thou the Lord.' Such will be how it is in the marriage of the blessed, and perfect will their disposition be towards those dearest to them.

CHAPTER SIXTEEN - THE CANAANITE WOMAN

Matthew 15:21-28

ONE OF THE OTHER

And his disciples came and begged him, saying, "Send her away, for she is crying after us." He answered, "I was sent only to the lost sheep of the house of Israel." - Matthew 15:23-24

Matthew tells us of the exchange between Jesus and a woman from Canaan. The woman's daughter was tormented by a demon, and she begged Jesus to help her. Can you imagine being this woman? Your daughter is very sick, possessed, and you've heard about this man who heals and casts out demons. You cry out to him, but he does not answer. His companions tell you to go away and ask the man to rebuff you and make you leave, and instead of showing the mercy and compassion you expect, he tells you he won't help you because you were born in the wrong place, to the wrong family, and practice the wrong religion. What would you say to an ER doctor who refuses to help you because of whom you are or how you worship?

Bishop Robert Barron speaks of this woman as being part of 'the other.' Those people whom we are obligated, as Christians, to care for: the stranger, the widow, and the orphan. This woman represents all those groups as well as the poor and all those outside of God's Church—those who practice other religions or no religion at all. Bishop Barron tells us that,

> We, the Church, are the Body of Christ. And so people come to us demanding food, sustenance, friendship, love, shelter, or liberation. Often we are tempted to do what Jesus does initially and what the disciples do: tell them to back off. We are overloaded, busy, and preoccupied. We can't be bothered. But the whole of the Christian life consists in remembering the suffering and need of the annoying other.[93]

Was Jesus really sent only to those of the House of Israel? Of course, he wasn't. We know this, and he knew it, but his followers did not understand yet that everyone was called to be saved by Christ, even this Canaanite woman. Jesus surely knew that he was going to heal her daughter, but he needed to make the point to his followers that even a woman from Canaan, an enemy of the Jews, could be brought into the House of the Lord.

Figure EE

How well do you remember this in your daily life? When we see 'the other,' the marginalized in our society, the sick and mentally ill, those of other faiths, do we look away? Do we pretend they don't exist? Do we close our eyes to their needs? Do we ignore their cries for help?

Even Jesus's closest followers were prepared to walk away, to send this woman home without her needs met and her desires fulfilled. How often do we do that? How many times have we put our wants and desires before those of others? Like the Priest and the Levite in the story of the Good Samaritan, how often do we cross the street, literally or figuratively?

Jesus instructs us, "whatever you did for one of these least brothers of mine, you did for me" (Matthew 25:40). When we turn away from one of God's children in

> **Whatever you did for one of these least brothers of mine, you did for me.**
> **Matthew 25:40**

need, we turn away from God, but when we help those who are less fortunate or sick or lonely or hungry or tired, we are helping God.

Moreover, the woman represents not just 'the other' but all others. She reminds us that we are part of a larger community. As Christians, we recognize that all people are God's children, part of his family, and part of the wider community that God wants to bring closer to himself. In the Canaanite woman, we see all people—the Gentiles and Jews, Christians and non-Christians, the believers and nonbelievers. Unfortunately, we often see others in terms of 'us' and 'they.' Jesus's "response isn't that different from the way many of us deal with people of other cultures, races, and religions."[94]

A NEW MINISTRY

"Lord, help me." And he answered, "It is not fair to take the children's bread and throw it to the dogs." She said, "Yes, Lord, yet even the dogs eat the crumbs that fall from their masters' table." - Matthew 15:25-27

Jesus sees this woman as an interruption to his day and to his mission. He has withdrawn to be alone, to pray, and to rest. His cousin has been beheaded. He has been rejected by his hometown and the religious leaders. He is annoyed, frustrated, and undoubtedly sad, yet here is a woman who will not leave him alone. Even his disciples see her as nothing more than a nuisance, someone to be dismissed and shooed away.

In our English interpretation, Jesus is comparing the woman to, perhaps even calling her, a dog. In our modern-day context, we are appalled and wonder how it is that this holy man, the Son of God, could be so cruel as to call her a dog, a being less than human. To better understand what Jesus is saying, we need to know that in Jesus's day, Gentiles—Non-Jews—were referred to as 'dogs.' In Greek, the word used for these people was *kuon*, which means 'wild cur.' They were seen as unclean and unworthy of God's promises.

Jesus acknowledges the ethnicity of the woman, reminding his followers she is unworthy of that which has been promised to God's chosen people. The woman does not disagree, saying to the Lord, "yet even the dogs eat the crumbs that fall from their masters' table" (Matthew 15:26). "She acknowledges what belongs to whom, what she is and what she is not— she is not a Jew, not of the house of Israel, and so not of his original mission, not one of his first choices to approach and save."[95]

Jesus and his followers have no pity on the woman or her daughter, yet Jesus and the woman have something in common. "They are both hurting, both looking for help, insight, and a way to survive in their worlds; no one else seems to care very much if either of them is taken care of adequately." [96] They are both suffering and in need of compassion and reassurance. This reassurance is exactly what the woman gives Jesus. This woman from another land, another religion, another mindset trusts that Jesus is who he says he is—Lord, Son of David—and that he can answer her prayers.

Upon hearing her words, Jesus reminds her and his followers that he has come to save the chosen people, not the Gentiles, and certainly not the Canaanites. Was this moment in Jesus's life a revelation to him just as it was a revelation to his followers? Did he truly know before this encounter that he was to save all people, or was this an epiphany for him? Some theologians believe Jesus's understanding of his mission grew as his ministry grew and

that this scene was a
moment of growth and
understanding for him, a
cairn for him along his
own journey. Remember,
it wasn't until after his
resurrection that Jesus
told the disciples, "Go,

Figure FF

therefore, and make disciples of all nations, baptizing them
in the name of the Father, and of the Son, and of the Holy
Spirit, teaching them to observe all that I have commanded
you" (Matthew 28:19-20).

This view of Christ's ministerial growth should be familiar
to us. We, too, grow in our ministries. We do not know
what the Lord has in mind for us. We learn what we are
called to do and be through prayer, scriptural study, and
intimate conversations with the Lord. By partaking in the
sacraments, by attending adoration, by reading the
scriptures and writings of the church, and through prayer,
we come to know how God wants us to minister, how he
wants us to spread his Word, and to whom we are to bring
his message. We follow the signs and markers God has
given us to move further along on our journey.

In telling Jesus that "even the dogs eat the crumbs that fall
from their masters' table." the woman is reminding him
that his mission is to bring all people to God, including
those who were deemed unworthy to the Jews. Perhaps her
words brought to Jesus's mind the words of Isaiah, "I am
coming to gather all nations and tongues; they shall come

and see my glory. I will place a sign among them; from them I will send survivors to the nations...to the distant coastlands which have never heard of my fame, or seen my glory; and they shall proclaim my glory among the nations" (Isaiah 66:18-19).

A MODEL OF FAITH

She said, "Yes, Lord, yet even the dogs eat the crumbs that fall from their masters' table. Then Jesus answered her, "O woman, great is your faith! Let it be done for you as you desire." - Matthew 15:27

The food that falls to the dogs is symbolic of the Bread of Life. "Though this bread will be offered first to the children of Israel, it will be denied to no one who asks for it."[97] It will be offered to all who have faith and accept Jesus for whom he is. This woman, not an Israelite, calls Jesus, *Lord.* She knows who she is and who he is, and as Jesus so often does, he

> "O woman, great is your faith! Let it be done for you as you desire." Matthew 15:27

turns upside-down his own acknowledgment that the food he offers is only for the chosen ones when he proclaims, "O woman, great is your faith! Let it be done for you as you desire" (Matthew 15:27). Using the same phrase he used to address his own mother, "O, woman" (John 2:4), Jesus elevates this woman to a person of honor and respect, one deserving of the Bread of Life. Jesus was not ignoring or denegrating the woman. He was using her as an example of faith! St. John chrystomdom taught "he put her off, that he might proclaim aloud this saying, that he might crown the woman."[98]

Jesus lets the woman, his disciples, and all who are present know the only thing separating God's people from everyone else is their faith in him. "Jesus is as saddened by the 'lack of faith' of his own neighbors and the 'little faith' of his own disciples as he is struck with admiration at the great faith of the Roman centurion and the Canaanite woman."[99] Jesus first let everyone know that this woman was not among the chosen, and then he gave her exactly what she asked for—healing for her daughter—and praised her for her great faith.

How great is your faith? Do you still believe when others tell you to stop asking or stop praying? Do you still believe when the devil tells you that you are not worthy? Do you still believe when it seems that even God himself refuses to answer your prayers? 7

A MODEL OF PERSISTENCE

"Have mercy on me, O Lord, Son of David." -
Matthew 15:22

The Canaanite Woman only wanted good. She wanted healing for her daughter. She wanted her daughter to be free of a demon tormenting her soul. We don't know how old the daughter was nor how long she suffered. All that we know is that her mother begged the Lord to heal her. This woman's story reminds me of another story, the story of a mother who prayed for seventeen years that her wayward son would repent and turn to God. St. Monica's "greatest sorrow" was when her son, Augustine, joined a religious cult. "For her, the spiritual death into which her son had fallen was more terrible than physical death."[100] Was not the soul of St. Augustine just as tormented by a demon? Was he not in need of healing? His mother, St. Monica, wanted only what was best for him; she wanted the demon to let go of his soul. "She petitioned the Lord even more with prayers and tears to hasten the day of Augustine's full conversion."[101] St. Ambrose, her spiritual guide, Monica was told that a child of so many tears could not be lost. How many tears had the Canaanite woman cried for her daughter? Whether the tears were few or infinitesimal, her faith, like that of St. Monica, pushed her to continue begging for the sake of her child.

Many mothers pray for healing for their children. So many people pray for healing of the body, mind, or soul for their loved ones. Like this woman and St. Monica, some pray for years without any sign that their prayers will be answered, but they continue to pray. Like the persistent widow in Jesus's parable, we need to persevere in prayer.

There was a judge in a certain town who neither feared God nor respected any human being. And a widow in that town used to come to him and say, "Render a just decision for me against my adversary." For a long time the judge was unwilling, but eventually he thought, "While it is true that I neither fear God nor respect any human being, because this widow keeps bothering me I shall deliver a just decision for her lest she finally come and strike me." (Luke 18:2-5)

Jesus knows this is hard. He knows that many will not have the faith to continue praying. After telling the parable of the widow, he lamented, "Will not God then secure the rights of his chosen ones who call out to him day and night? Will he be slow to answer them? I tell you, he will see to it that justice is done for them speedily. But when the Son of Man comes, will he find faith on earth?" (Luke 18:7-8). Like the widow in his parable, Jesus saw the Canaanite woman's persistence, recognized her faith, and healed her child.

Be a person of perseverance and faith. Do not lose hope even when things look bleak, even when you feel like you are being kicked around like a dog. "For in hope we were saved. Now

> **But if we hope for what we do not see, we wait with endurance (Romans 8:25).**

hope that sees for itself is not hope. For who hopes for what one sees? But if we hope for what we do not see, we wait with endurance" (Romans 8:24-25).

Have patience and know that God listens and answers all your prayers. Know that he wants what is good for you and that he hears when you pray for what is good and just. Know that our will is not always his will but "all things work for good for those who love God" (Romans 8:28).

CHAPTER SEVENTEEN - THE HEMORRHAGING WOMAN

Mark 5:24-34

LOST AND AFRAID

Now there was a woman who had been suffering from hemorrhages for twelve years. [26] She had endured much under many physicians, and had spent all that she had; and she was no better, but rather grew worse. [27] She had heard about Jesus, and came up behind him in the crowd and touched his cloak, [28] for she said, "If I but touch his clothes, I will be made well." - Mark 5:25-28

How my heart aches when I hear this story. For months after the birth of our third child, I suffered in the same way as this woman. I can't even imagine years of this affliction; and for her, the suffering was more than physical suffering. She was also suffering mentally and spiritually, for bleeding of any kind was seen as unclean. This meant she was separated from her family and friends, and she was not allowed in the temple. She was estranged from everyone, including God. To touch Jesus would have been to make him unclean as well, but like so many who wished for healing, she understood the power of touch.

A great crowd of his disciples and a large number of the people from all Judea and Jerusalem and the coastal region of Tyre and Sidon came to hear him and to be healed of their diseases; and even those who were tormented by unclean spirits were cured. Everyone in the crowd sought to touch him because power came forth from him and healed them all. - Luke 6:17-19

I have very vivid memories of being a nine-year-old child standing near a barrier at Andrews Air Force Base when Pope John Paul II landed and stepped off his plane in my home state of Maryland. It was 1979, and he was concluding his first trip to the United States with a visit to the White House and the celebration of Mass on the National Mall. I recall that His Holiness landed in the evening. I was with my mother and our good friends and neighbors, the LeBlancs. Mr. LeBlanc was the pilot of Air Force One, and they had taken us as their guests to witness this historic moment.

As the Pope walked across the tarmac, I had the sudden desire to touch him, at the very least, to touch the hem of his robe, much like the hemorrhaging woman's desire to touch the hem of Jesus's cloak. I remember squatting down and reaching beneath the barrier, stretching my arm across the pavement, and touching the soft white cloth that floated by. When I stood, I could not see my mother or our friends. I looked and looked, trying to be strong and brave, and I was, until another mother saw me and asked if I was lost. I burst into tears, and she stood with me, aside from the crowd and waited for my mother to find me.

Sometimes, when I gaze at the picture hanging in my bedroom, a snapshot of the mural of the hemorrhaging woman which hangs in the Duc in Altum Church in Magdala, I see my nine-year-old hand in the place of the woman's wrinkled one. I understand her desire to touch Jesus's cloak, and for a brief time, I understand her fear and loneliness. I was without my mother for minutes, alone and looking for help, asking the other mother to stay with me, to help me find my mom. The hemorrhaging woman had nobody. She had been ostracized for twelve years. I can imagine that she felt lost, alone, and afraid. And then word came to her of this man of God who could perform miracles, who could heal people of their afflictions. She knew all she had to do was get close enough to touch his clothes. There was no question in her mind, "If I but touch his clothes, I will be made well" (Mark 5:25-28). What remarkable courage and faith!

Figure GG

How could this woman have known Jesus could and would heal her? How did she know all she needed to do was touch his cloak? There is only one answer. She had immeasurable faith. She knew Jesus was the answer to all her questions, all her years of suffering. She knew Jesus had the power to make her whole, bring her back into society, take away her pain—both physical and emotional—and bring her back into the fold of his people. She knew that even the smallest action on her part would be enough for Jesus to feel her presence and her needs and to heal her.

Sometimes we think that we aren't enough, that our actions aren't enough, that our pain and suffering go unnoticed; but our God is a merciful and loving God. He declared to Jeremiah, "I will restore you to health and heal your wounds" (Jeremiah 30:17). Whether we are suffering from a physical affliction, a mental one, or a spiritual one, all we need to have is faith; and all we need to do is reach out and touch the Lord, and he will know that we are there, asking for his help.

THE IMMEDIACY OF GOD

And immediately the hemorrhage ceased; and she felt in her body that she was healed of her disease. And Jesus, perceiving in himself that power had gone forth from him, immediately turned about in the crowd, and said, "Who touched my garments?" - Mark 5:30

"Jesus hears the prayer of faith, expressed in words…the Canaanite woman…or in silence…the woman with a hemorrhage who touches his clothes."[102] This daughter of God did not audibly ask Jesus for help, yet she trusted that she could be healed through touch. She silently reached through the crowd and touched his cloak, and she was immediately healed. "Mark, in his repeated use of the word 'immediately,' is trying to get across the point that Jesus wastes no time. He is in a hurry to draw people into this new realm of the kingdom."[103]

Mark used the word 'immediately' forty-one times in his Gospel, an average of two times per chapter, giving "a sense of a rapid-fire narrative" which highlights the importance of the works Jesus performed. Jesus does not waste time! His work within us begins the moment we seek his help.[104] The woman was healed instantly and felt the healing instantly. She knew as soon as she touched Jesus that her disease was gone. Likewise, Jesus knew as soon as she touched his cloak that she had been healed. How amazing that must have been!

It seems we so often must wait for answers, for proof, for healing. We go to a doctor, endure tests, wait for a diagnosis, take medicine, or undergo a procedure and then must wait for healing or relief. Even in our faith journey, we spend our lives waiting to reach that pivotal time and place where we know for sure that we are saved, that God has healed all our afflictions of mind, body, and soul. Yet Jesus knows us and loves us immediately. He begins healing us the instant we ask for help even if takes years for us to see or feel his healing touch. Like a parent who longs to free her child of pain, God longs to free his sons and daughters of pain. He "comes with a strength that turns out to be tender and affectionate, gentle and meek…as if we too were his sons and daughters."[105] And of course, that's exactly who we are.

DAUGTER OF GOD - HUMBLE BEFORE THE LORD

He looked all around to see who had done it. But the woman, knowing what had happened to her, came in fear and trembling, fell down before him, and told him the whole truth. He said to her, "Daughter, your faith has made you well; go in peace, and be healed of your disease."
- Mark 5:32-34

The Catechism tells us that "our experiences of evil and suffering, injustice, and death, seem to contradict the Good News; they can shake our faith and become a temptation against it."[106] Yet our Father in Heaven loves us greatly and feels our pain. "This is the meaning, ultimately, of the deliverance and the healings worked by Jesus…He comes to take his children back." [107] In Mark's story of the hemorrhaging woman, Jesus uses the suffering of this daughter of God and, with mercy and compassion, heals her body and soul. He calls her "Daughter" and heals her, just as in the story where Jesus heals a crippled woman, calling her "a daughter of Abraham" (Luke 13:16). In both cases, Jesus calls the women "daughter" and says to her, "O, woman," thus elevating the stature of all women. We are all daughters of God.

The hemorrhaging woman went before Jesus, in fear and trembling, and humbly fell before him. She did not run away in either shame or triumph. She did not deny what she had done. She faced Jesus with humility. And Jesus called her "daughter"'and told her she was healed. Jesus confirmed that he was "sent to the lost sheep of the house of Israel and now to anyone who approaches him in hope, in need, and in faith, to anyone who humbles himself or herself before him and acknowledges his mission."[108]

The concept of being a child of God is simple and humble.[109] As the sons and daughters of God, we are called to humble ourselves and accept God's will in our lives. We are called to Jesus and called to be like Jesus. "Come to me, all you who are weary and find life burdensome, and I will refresh you. Take my yoke upon your shoulders and learn from me, for I am

> "Come to me, all you who are weary and find life burdensome, and I will refresh you" (Matthew 11:25).

gentle and humble of heart. Your souls will find rest, for my yoke is easy and my burden light" (Matthew 11:25-30). The yoke of Jesus is gentle and humble, close to the earth, human and merciful, tender as a mother for a child, a father for a newborn, a grandparent with grandchildren. In this revelation, this relationship, we will find rest, comfort, care, protection, and light-heartedness.[110] We are to be yoked, or tethered, to Jesus so that he may share in our sufferings and burdens. He wants to be close enough to us that we can reach out, beneath the barrier, through the crowd, and touch him, even if all we can reach is the hem of his cloak.

We must, daily, reach for Jesus. We must try to touch him. We must humble ourselves before him, bowing to the ground, falling upon our knees, so that we are at the level of his feet, the hem of his cloak. We do these things not to grovel or be pitied but so that Jesus can elevate us and lift us up to where he wants us to be in life. We need to make ourselves low so we can rise to our proper place as daughters of God.

Remember this the next time you are questioning who you are or where you belong. You are a daughter of God. You are special, you are loved, and you may approach the Lord humbly, with your needs, as his daughter. Then you will be fed, "not by scraps but with the very Bread of Heaven."[111]

CHAPTER EIGHTEEN - PHOTINA, THE WOMAN AT THE WELL

John 4:1-42

THIRSTY FOR MORE

Jesus said to her, "Everyone who drinks of this water will be thirsty again, but those who drink of the water that I will give them will never be thirsty. The water that I will give will become in them a spring of water gushing up to eternal life." The woman said to him, "Sir, give me this water, so that I may never be thirsty or have to keep coming here to draw water." - John 4:13-15

It was noon, and a woman from Samaria, known by Biblical scholars as Photina (according to Greek tradition and later proclaimed a martyr by Cardinal Cesare Baronius), was drawing water at the well. Had Jesus not had the foresight of God, he still would have known something was not right with the woman. Why was she drawing water at noon, in the heat of the day, and not in the coolness of the morning when the other women visited with each other while drawing water for their daily chores? This is our first clue that Photina needs more than water. She, like the hemorrhaging woman, is an outcast, someone ostracized from her friends, family, and neighbors. She visits the well when there is nobody else around, when she can be alone to fetch the water she will need for the day. Photina does not know Jesus. As a Samaritan, she would be familiar with the Jewish God,* but all she knows about this man is that he is a Jew, and he is asking her for a drink, something unheard of. She has three things against her from the start—she is without companions, she is a woman, and she is a Samaritan. Yet Jesus is waiting for her.

Figure HH

Once again, Jesus elevates the status of a woman, but he does more than that. In speaking to Photina, he sees her as a human with dignity. In asking to share in the water she is drawing, perhaps drinking from the same cup, he recognizes her as a person of worth, not just a Samaritan. Jesus was thirsty, but not for water. According to St. Augustine, Jesus was thirsting for her faith.[112] As Pope

---

* Jews and Samarians worshipped the same God, but the Samaritans worshipped at a temple on Mount Gerizim, not in Jerusalem. The Jews saw the Samaritans as lost souls, contaminated by pagan gods.

Francis said, "Jesus' thirst was not so much for water, but for the encounter with a parched soul. Jesus needed to encounter the Samaritan woman in order to open her heart: he asks for a drink so as to bring to light her own thirst."[113]

We all thirst. We thirst not just for liquid nourishment but for spiritual nourishment, and that is exactly what Jesus offers to Photina and to us. He tells her, "Everyone who drinks of this water will be thirsty again, but those who drink of the water that I will give them will never be thirsty. The water that I will give will become in them a spring of water gushing up to eternal life" (John 4: 13-15). Photina responds in the same way we should respond, "Sir, give me this water, so that I may never be thirsty." What is this water? The answer is

> "Sir, give me this water, so that I may never be thirsty" (John 4:15).

multifold, for the water Jesus gives is the living water of his Spirit but also his mercy, his compassion, and his love. What this woman has yet to understand is that "to the soul of an adorer, the Real Presence of Christ is like a fountain of living water in a dry and arid land."[114]

There are two places in the Bible, both in John's Gospel, where Jesus makes known that he is thirsty. The first is here, when he asks for a drink. The second is from the cross when Jesus says, "I thirst" (John 19:28). In both instances, Jesus's request is followed by a gushing of water. Here, he describes the water he will give as "water gushing up to eternal life." On the cross, Jesus is given a drink, bows his head, and dies, preceding the piercing of his side when "at once there came out blood and water" (John 19:34).

What is the relation of one to the other? First, Jesus asks for a drink; then, Jesus becomes the source of the life-giving water. The water that gushes from Jesus's side symbolizes the same life-giving water that he offered the woman. But what is this living water? John tells us that at the Festival of Booths, "Jesus stood up and proclaimed, 'If any one thirsts, let him come to me and drink. He who believes in me,' as the scripture has said, 'Out of his heart shall flow rivers of living water'" (John 7:37-38). The water of eternal life is the Holy Spirit. Jesus is the source of living water coming from the well, and we are his jars, the carriers of the water to those who thirst. Liike Photina, who first met Jesus at the well, we thirst; like the woman who met Jesus and had her thirst satisfied, we are to take the living water to everyone we know, proclaiming the works of Christ.

> **"If any one thirsts, let him come to me and drink" (John 7:37).**

THE TRUE BRIDEGROOM

Jesus said to her, "Go, call your husband, and come back." The woman answered him, "I have no husband." Jesus said to her, "You are right in saying, 'I have no husband'; for you have had five husbands, and the one you have now is not your husband. What you have said is true!" - John 4:16-17

Photina has often been looked down upon for being a sinner, having had five husbands and then living with a man who was not her husband. However, in those days, women had no say in a divorce. It was completely up to the husband to divorce the wife, and she was cast out with no choice. Perhaps this outspoken woman was seen as troublesome by her husbands. Maybe they weren't happy with someone who didn't succumb to life as a docile wife. Or perhaps, the woman wasn't divorced at all. Maybe, following Mosaic law, she was widowed and forced to remarry five times. The man she was with when she met Jesus may not have been considered her lawful husband because she chose someone outside of her husband's kin. Whatever the reason, Photina is not accepted within her community, but Jesus accepts her, loves her, and offers to quench her thirst when they meet at Jacob's well.

It's not by chance that this meeting takes place at a well—a true cairn for the Jewish people. Abraham's servant met Rebekah, whom he chose as Issacs's wife, at a well. Jacob met Rachel at this same well in Samaria. Moses encountered his father-in-law at a well, leading to his marriage to Zipporah. Here, it is at a well that Jesus asks about the woman's husband and tells her of the true bridegroom. The meeting at the well is meant to remind us that Jesus is the bridegroom, and the Samaritans are invited to be part of the Church—the bride of Christ.

Jesus and Photina have quite the exchange. He not only asks for a drink and offers her the water of eternal life, he proceeds to tell her that he knows she has had five husbands! Why is this important? Here, Jesus reminds Photina of the history of the Samaritans and how they cut themselves off from the true God, the God of Israel. After Israel's defeat to Assyria, the king of Assyria brought people from five different nations into the land of Samaria (2 Kings 17:24). These people brought with them their foreign gods "and put them in the shrines of the high places which the Samaritans had made" (2 Kings 17:29). "Jesus desires the 'hour that is coming' when he inaugurates the New Covenant and Israel can return and once again be wed to her true husband and Lord."[115]

Throughout the Old and New Testaments, we hear of the Bridegroom and the Wedding Feast of the Lamb. The prophet Hosea described God as the husband of Israel. "And in that day, says the Lord, you will call me, 'My Husband'" (Hosea 2:16), referring to the coming of the Messiah and the new Kingdom of God. It was John the Baptist who first referred to Jesus as, "He who has the bride is the bridegroom" (John 3:29), proclaiming that the new kingdom has arrived, and Jesus is the bridegroom coming to claim his bride—the people of God, the Church. "On the cross, Jesus, the heavenly Bridegroom, offers himself in a spousal gift of self-giving love."[116] Jesus, as the Bridegroom of the new Kingdom of God, will be the last husband of the woman, for he has come to all people, including the Samaritans.

We are all called to be brides of Christ, not just the religious women and men who profess vows of marriage to the

Church. We are all called to be a part of this intimate relationship, to love Jesus in the self-sacrificing love of a spouse. "Christ loved the church and gave himself up for her, that he might sanctify her, having cleansed her by the washing of water with the word, that he might present the church to himself in splendor, without spot or wrinkle or any such thing, that she might be holy and without blemish" (Ephesians 5:25-27). We are called to join Jesus at his table in Heaven, to be washed with the living water and the Word, where we will celebrate the eternal feast of the Bridegroom and His Holy Church—the people of God.

THE SPIRIT OF LIFE AND TRUTH

"But the hour is coming, and is now here, when the true worshipers will worship the Father in spirit and truth, for the Father seeks such as these to worship him. - John 4:25.

Jesus revealed much to Photina, a non-Jew, an outcast, a woman with five husbands and no friends. He told her that he is the living water, he is the Bridegroom, and he will send forth his Spirit. If she still does not get it, he sums it up with the words, "I am." First spoken to Moses on Mt. Sinai, God revealed his name as "I am Who Am" (Exodus 3:14). Each time Jesus says the words, "I am" in the Gospel, he is revealing that he is God and that what he is saying is coming directly from the mouth of God.

> "For where two or three are gathered in my name, I am there among them." (Matthew 18:20)
> "Jesus said, "I am; and 'you will see the Son of Man seated at the right hand of the Power,' and 'coming with the clouds of heaven.'" Mark 14:62
> "All of them asked, 'Are you, then, the Son of God?' He said to them, 'You say that I am.'." (Luke 22:70)
> "Jesus said to them, 'I am the bread of life. Whoever comes to me will never be hungry, and whoever believes in me will never be thirsty'." (John 6:35)

How blessed Photina was to hear this pronouncement straight from the mouth of God! "I am the one who is speaking to you." Can you imagine her shock and then her joy at hearing these words? She had an open dialogue with the Lord, but you know what? You can have one, too! You can speak openly to the Lord. You can ask him questions, tell him your doubts, your troubles, and your fears. You can give Jesus that which he seeks—your attention, your burdens, and your faith—and Jesus will speak back. He will answer your prayers. He will reassure you. He will bring you joy. All you need to do is satisfy his thirst, and he, through the work of his Spirit, will satisfy yours.

Are you thirsting? Are you in need of the Holy Spirit, the life-giving waters of Jesus? Do you have a relationship with the Holy Spirit? For many, that's the one being in the Trinity they find the hardest to understand or relate to. For years, I didn't pay any attention to the Holy Spirit at all. I understood that, through Confirmation, I was to develop a deeper relationship with the Holy Spirit, but what is he or she or it? How do we have a relationship with a being we can't even conceptualize?

I think the best way to think about the Holy Spirit is that it is the part of God that breathes into us life and truth. Job so beautifully sums it up by proclaiming, "The Spirit of God made me and the breath of the Almighty has given me life" (Job 33:4). The Creed tells us that the Holy Spirit is the "Giver of Life." To the woman at the well, Jesus said, "God is spirit, and those who worship him must worship in spirit and truth" (John 4:24). He speaks those same words to us. We must use the gifts of the Spirit—wisdom, understanding, counsel, fortitude, knowledge, piety, and fear of the Lord—to spread the truth.

AN EVANGELIST FOR CHRIST

Then the woman left her water jar and went back to the city. She said to the people, "Come and see a man who told me everything I have ever done! He cannot be the Messiah, can he?" …Many Samaritans from that city believed in him because of the woman's testimony, "He told me everything I have ever done." So when the Samaritans came to him, they asked him to stay with them; and he stayed there two days. And many more believed because of his word. They said to the woman, "It is no longer because of what you said that we believe, for we have heard for ourselves, and we know that this is truly the Savior of the world." - John 4:28-30; 39-41

Photina became the evangelist to her fellow villagers who, through her, came to know Jesus as the Savior of the world. [117] St. Chrysostom said, "Observe her zeal and wisdom. She came to draw water, and when she had lighted upon the true Well, she after that despised the material one."[118] She tells the villagers, the same people she had been avoiding, "Come see a man who told me all that I ever did. Could this be the Christ?" (John 4:29). The villagers listened to her and went out to seek Jesus, and "many Samaritans from that city believed in him because of the woman's testimony" (John 4:39). They believed not only because of her words but because she drank of the living water. She was filled with the Holy Spirit.

We must pray that God will fill us with the Holy Spirit. We must talk to the Lord, listen to him, and tell others about him. We must proclaim the Good News, telling everyone that Jesus is the Christ. We must follow the example of Photina. When we truly know Jesus, and when we drink of the living water, we should be so full of zeal that we can't help but spread the news that Jesus is Messiah, the Son of God. We can be the cairns for others who are seeking their path to the Lord!

SPREADING THE WORD OF GOD'S KINGDOM
Martha, Mary, and Mary Magdalene

CHAPTER NINETEEN - MARTHA AND MARY

Luke 10:38-42; John 11:1-12:8

SISTERS IN FAITH AND ACTION

Martha was distracted by her many tasks; so she came to him and asked, "Lord, do you not care that my sister has left me to do all the work by myself? Tell her then to help me." But the Lord answered her, "Martha, Martha, you are worried and distracted by many things; there is need of only one thing. Mary has chosen the better part, which will not be taken away from her." - Luke 10:40-42

Most people have heard the story of Martha and Mary welcoming Jesus into their home. There has long been a debate among many women about the actions of the two sisters. While Jesus says that Mary, who sat at his feet and listened to him preach, chose the better part, many ask, but what about the dinner Martha was preparing for Jesus? Did he not appreciate her efforts? Are we to live lives of meditative prayer and forsake all the necessary tasks that are to be done?

In his Angelus on 21 July, 2019, Pope Francis told the listeners,

Saint Luke shows the prayerful attitude of the believer, who is able to be in the Teacher's presence to listen to him and be in harmony with him. It means pausing a few minutes during the day to gather yourself in silence, to make room for the Lord who 'is passing' and to find the courage to stay somewhat 'on the sidelines' with him, in order to return later with serenity and strength, to everyday matters.[119]

We are all called to do this—to spend quiet time with the Lord, talking to him and listening to him, just as Mary did. Pope Francis said that Jesus is telling us, "Do not allow yourselves to be overwhelmed by things to do, but first and foremost listen to the Lord's voice."[120] Sitting at the feet of the Lord, hearing his words, and meditating on his message is the place

> **"Do not allow yourselves to be overwhelmed by things to do, but first and foremost listen to the Lord's voice" (Pope Francis).**

that expresses our true humility and adoration of Jesus.[121] It is the place where we should find ourselves often.

At the same time, we have Martha, the one who received Jesus and welcomed him into their home through action. Pope Francis recognized that Martha had the "charism of hospitality," a truly good and necessary quality when used with the right attitude. While Mary listened to Jesus, Martha was completely caught up in serving her guests, anxious over the work that needed to be done rather than pausing to be in the moment with the Lord. This is why Jesus says to her: "Martha, Martha, you are anxious and troubled about many things" (Luke 10:41). Jesus is not condemning the attitude of service, but rather the stress which one places on herself when tending to her service.[122]

It was not Martha's cooking or cleaning or preparing the table for the meal that was wrong. It was her anxiousness and troubling thoughts that were getting in the way. She was not able to enjoy the Lord's company because she was worrying too much about the logistics of the evening. I can certainly relate to that! Our family loves to entertain. We enjoy nothing more than opening our home to guests for any and all occasions. Every Christmas, we hold a mother-daughter cookie swap for which I provide an entire three

Figure 11

or four course sit-down dinner, complete with small gifts for each guest, and of course, a platter of carefully decorated sugar cookies for each family to take home with them. There have been many times when I have let the preparations get in the way of having a good time,

enjoying our friendships, and just being in the moment. Over the years, I've learned how to spread out the preparations over a few months, to choose easy-to-prepare meals, and to have the tables ready the day before, taking my time and not feeling pressured. I've also learned to ask my daughters for help, especially ahead of time, something Martha could have done. These actions allow me to enjoy visiting with our guests and listening to their stories, much like Mary did at the feet of our Lord. Do I still become anxious at times when this or that doesn't turn out right? Of course, but I try to remind myself that my guests come for the same reason we hold the event—to be among friends and enjoy the evening.

It's not wrong to be a Martha just as it's perfectly all right to be a Mary. The key is not to worry or be anxious. We fail to see or hear the Lord when we are too worried, too busy, or too distracted. "Martha was undoubtedly full of goodwill in wanting to serve the Lord, but... Martha misses [the] communication from the Lord because she is too distracted, and often this is true for us."[123] We must let the Lord guide us and know that he is sharing in our burdens. Before any work or service or event we are planning, we must pray that our actions will be worthy of God and that we will know when to serve, when to pray, when to listen, and how to do all at the same time.

When faced with a challenging task or a task I don't want to do (like the seventh load of laundry over the course of a day), it often helps if I remind myself that all my works should be a form of prayer. Before giving into anxiety, I try to think of an intention and offer the work as a sacrificial prayer. I remind myself that I can serve my family, friends, and community and still make time for prayer—both mediative and active. We need to find balance in our lives—the perfect combination of both service and prayer.

STRENGTH AND DIGNITY

When Martha heard that Jesus was coming, she went and met him, while Mary stayed at home. Martha said to Jesus, "Lord, if you had been here, my brother would not have died. But even now I know that God will give you whatever you ask of him." - John 11:20-23

A few years ago, one of the Bible study groups that I lead discussed Martha and Mary. One of the women stood up for Martha, saying that sometimes we need the Marthas more than we need the Marys. Even Jesus needed Martha to take charge at one point. After all, while Mary wept over her brother's body as he lay in the tomb, it was Martha who went in search of the Lord, asking for her brother to be raised. While Mary, earlier in the Bible, seems to have it all figured out as she sits silently and attentively at the feet of the Lord, we see a need at times for Martha to come in and take charge.

Martha believes *even now* after her brother has already died, that Jesus can help them. Jesus is there *even now*. "Even now, when life has not turned out as I imagined. Even now, when I do not understand the difficulties or sufferings I face. Even now, when things do make sense, and I feel forgotten...overwhelmed, anxious, or lonely," Jesus is here.[124]

Here, it seems that Martha is the strong one, the one who knows what actions need to be done, the one who boldly goes to seek help from the Lord as the contemplative one mourns with grief. Martha finds Jesus and greets him in the same blunt way that she confronted him earlier in her home. She does not mince words, even to Jesus. She trusts him to listen to her and tend to her needs. "Martha's fierce honesty also reminds us that Jesus included strong women among his circle of friends."[125] Martha is much like the woman described in Proverbs as the Capable Wife—she buys the good field and plants the fruit, knows when her merchandize is profitable, puts her hands to the distaff and the spindle, opens her hand to the poor, is not afraid when it snows. She makes herself and her family clothing, and clothes herself with strength and dignity. "She looks well to the ways of her household, and does not eat the bread of idleness" (Proverbs 31).

Martha, like the Capable Wife, knows what needs to be done, and she does it. She does not waste time and does not let obstacles stand in her way, even death. Martha is a doer. She tends to the tasks at hand, springs into action when something needs to be taken care of, and expects others to do the same. She does not sit idle and does not wait for others to volunteer. She takes charge and makes things happen.

We cannot raise people from the dead, just as Mary and Martha could not raise their brother, but we can and should have the faith that Martha had that we all will be raised on the last day. We can rest assured that Jesus can perform miracles, that he can save people from death—physical and spiritual. We cannot be all things to all people. Few of us have the wisdom of Solomon, and we all have weaknesses. Yet we can strive to be strong in our faith. We can work hard and pray hard. We can take charge when it is necessary and know that God can and does give us whatever we ask.

Let us not forget, though, how Mary's reaction to the arrival of the Lord affected the scene. "When Jesus saw her weeping, he was greatly disturbed in spirit and deeply moved. He said, 'Where have you laid him?' They said to him, 'Lord, come and see.' Jesus wept" (John 11:33-35).

Figure JJ

This is the shortest and perhaps the most emotional passage in the Bible. In its simplicity, that one sentence tells us all we need to know about Jesus's love for this family. Jesus, who knows he will bring Lazarus back from the dead, who has preached endlessly on the resurrection of the body, who knows this world is the not the end for us, is moved to human tears by the death of his friend, but even more so by Mary's tears. This woman, whom we will see meant so much to Jesus, who sat at his feet, who anointed him for burial, who stood at the cross, who shed countless tears for the Lord, moved Jesus to weep.

How often have you been in a situation where someone begins to cry, and without being able to stop yourself, you cry, too? We're beings of empathy. We feel things, often deeply. Like us, Jesus was human, a being of empathy. He shared our same emotions. We should never forget, when we go to Jesus in our times of distress and despair, he understands, and he felt distress and despair, too. Mary wept, and the Lord wept, and when we are at our lowest, the Lord, in solidarity with our sadness, weeps with us. Let us always remember at these times the words Jesus prayed at Lazarus's tomb, "Father, I thank you that you have heard me. I know that you always hear me" (John 11:41-42).

SPENDING TIME WITH THE LORD

Six days before the Passover Jesus came to Bethany, the home of Lazarus, whom he had raised from the dead. There they gave a dinner for him. Martha served, and Lazarus was one of those at the table with him. Mary took a pound of costly perfume made of pure nard, anointed Jesus' feet, and wiped them with her hair. The house was filled with the fragrance of the perfume. But Judas Iscariot…said, "Why was this perfume not sold for three hundred denarii and the money given to the poor?"…Jesus said, "Leave her alone. She bought it so that she might keep it for the day of my burial. You always have the poor with you, but you do not always have me."
- John 12:1-8

Once again, we see Martha slaving away while Mary sits at the feet of our Lord. Perhaps, after Jesus's admonishment earlier in the Gospels and his raising of Lazarus, Martha serves now with joy. There doesn't seem to be any animosity this time, just the need to serve. Things are different now, and we can feel it as we read the passage. This scene, though the setting is the same as before, is more ominous. Jesus's time with them was nearing the end.

It was six days before Passover, and one day before Jesus would enter the city to the swaying of palms and the cries of, "Hosanna! Blessed is the one who comes in the name of the Lord" (John 12:13). By this time, Jesus has mentioned several times to his followers the hour of his death is near. Judas is getting testy, and Mary anoints Jesus with the perfumed oil of the burial rite. Though they do not know when, they recognize the time is coming to say goodbye. Mary lavishes Jesus with perfumed oil, the scent of which fills the whole house, signifying Mary's overwhelming love and generosity for Jesus. [126] Judas responds with anger and disgust, but Jesus praises Mary for recognizing his time with them is ending.

How do we treat our time with Jesus? Do we rush through prayer, daydream during Mass, or put off the Sacrament of Reconciliation? Do we live like our own time on earth is eternal, or do we recognize we only have so much time to get it right, listen to Jesus, serve him well, and lavish him with our love and generosity? Do we give Jesus the time and attention he deserves? Do we take the time each day to appreciate all God has given to us and bask in the gift of life?

THE PROPER BALANCE

Within each of us lies a Martha or a Mary; however, those who possess the characteristics of both women are truly the smart ones, the ones who understand that life is a balance. In Luke's story of Martha cooking and cleaning while Mary sits at the feet of Jesus, Martha always seems to get the bad rap, but I would argue that the world needs both Marthas and Marys.

> **The world needs both Marthas and Marys.**

The Marthas among us (regardless of the names) are doers. They are workers, inventors, crafters, movers, and shakers. They teach, preach, and entertain. They stand up for what is right. They jump in and take over. They lead and command. They are Girl Scout Leaders and PTA Presidents and ethical politicians and advocates for those in need. They make things happen.

Marys are quiet, introspective, meditative, cautious, and prayerful. They remind us to slow down, smell the roses, and enjoy the little things in life. They are gentle, kind, and compassionate. They work quietly behind the scenes in places like classrooms, St. Vincent de Paul centers, churches, soup kitchens, and emergency services. They typically do as they are asked, always ready to do the Lord's bidding.

"For everything there is a season, and a time for every matter under heaven" (Ecclesiastes 3:1). There is a time for each of us to be a Martha and a time for each of us to be a Mary. Throughout this chapter, we have seen how both Martha and Mary loved and honored the Lord. Neither was wholly wrong or wholly right, but they complimented each other in their approaches to Jesus. Our goal should be to emulate both Martha and Mary. Pope Francis said that "the wisdom of the heart lies precisely in knowing how to combine these two elements: contemplation and action" (emphasis by the Pope).[127] He said Mary and Martha both show us the path—

> **"The wisdom of the heart lies precisely in knowing how to combine these two elements: contemplation and action" (Pope Francis).**

that we must listen at the feet of Jesus and be "attentive and ready in hospitality, when he passes and knocks at our door, with the face of a friend who needs a moment of rest and fraternity."[128]

A dear friend of mine is the perfect example of this. She is hard-working, kind, loving, compassionate, a volunteer, an advocate for those in need, and a deeply prayerful and meditative person. For a few years, she was embroiled in a battle with cancer, and it looks like she has won the battle. She understands that there are times when we need to lead and times when we need to be led. Her faith in action has always been an inspiration to everyone who knows her, and her time spent battling this disease was no exception. She was fighting to survive while taking advantage of the many quiet moments for prayer and reflection. In fact, every time we got together, and I mentioned someone who was struggling, someone who was sick or in pain, someone who was discerning, or any concern of my own, she whipped out her little pocket notebook and turned to the bookmarked page where she last wrote. "Give me their names and the intention," she always asked, and I held back tears as she hurriedly wrote down the information. She was putting her quiet, meditative prayer life into action. She was going to the Lord with her prayers and my prayers and the prayers of every person who, like me, mentioned someone or something in need. She taught me how to be both Martha and Mary. She was a cairn on my continuing journey.

CHAPTER TWENTY - MARY MAGDALENE AND MARY OF BETHANY

Matthew 27:55-61; 28:1-10; Mark 15:40-47; 16:1-11; Luke 7:36-50; 8:1-3; 10:38-42; 24:10; John 11:1-44;12:1-8; 19:25-27; 20:11-18

> *The twelve were with him, as well as some women who had been cured of evil spirits and infirmities: Mary, called Magdalene, from whom seven demons had gone out, and Joanna, the wife of Herod's steward Chuza, and Susanna, and many others, who provided for them out of their resources.* - Luke 8:2-3

At the beginning of the twentieth century, especially within modern feminist circles, there arose a great debate about exactly whom Mary Magdalene was. She has been identified as the sinful woman who anointed Jesus's feet with oil and dried them with her tears (at the beginning of his ministry), as Mary of Magdala who was cured of possession by seven demons, and as Mary, the sister of Martha and Lazarus. She has been mistaken for the adulterous woman and a prostitute.

Mary of Magdala is mentioned by name four times in the Bible: in the context of a woman cured of possession, a trusted follower of Jesus who helped finance his ministry, one of those at the foot of the cross, and the first person to see the Risen Christ.

For years, I bristled at the thought that Mary of Bethany was the sinful woman, crying at Jesus's feet, and I never understood why she would have been confused with Mary, Martha's sister, when the two lived at opposite ends of the country. I, like many, pictured her as the adulterous woman or a prostitute. Like so many of my contemporizes, I did not know who the real Mary Magdalene was.

However, I have come to understand, with the help of the early Church Fathers and theologians, who Mary is. I fully believe the penitent woman who appears at Jesus's feet early in the Gospels, Mary of Bethany, and Mary of Magdala are the same person. The most beautiful thing about this revelation is that it does not detract in the slightest from the holy woman we now know as St. Mary Magdalene. Rather, it affirms her holiness and the stark transformation she made from sinner to saint.

In his book, *Saint Mary Magdalene*, Father Sean Davidson, a Magdalene scholar, reveals the clues on which he contends that Mary Magdalene is none other than the penitent woman at the feet of Jesus, Mary the benefactress of Jesus's ministry, and Mary, sister of Martha and Lazarus. This last Mary is simply called 'Mary' in the Bible—not Mary of Bethany—with no explanation as to whom she was. No explanation was needed. The Apostles and early Church fathers knew exactly who Mary was. Father Davidson makes it clear, using writings of the early Church Fathers, that these three women are all Mary Magdalene, born in or near Bethany but living in Magdala when she first encountered Christ, and he healed her of seven demons.

The theological authority of intellectual giants such as Saint Augustine and Pope Saint Gregory the Great was, until recently, sufficient to convince the entire Catholic Church that the evangelists were not speaking of three different women but one woman. Raban Maur, in his ninth-century work on the life of Saint Mary Magdalene, confirmed the universal acceptance of her identity—not only her identity but also her escape to France were well known to all of Christendom.[129] It was not until the sixteenth century, with the advent of Protestantism, that non-Catholics began to question Mary's identity. Among those who protested this division of identities was Saint Thomas More, a man deeply devoted to the traditional image of Mary Magdalene. For the average Catholic, there was no question or debate about the identity of Mary Magdalene until the Twentieth Century. For centuries the Tridentine liturgy proclaimed that all three women were one in the same.[130]

A LOST SOUL

...and standing behind him at his feet, weeping, she began to wet his feet with her tears, and wiped them with the hair of her head, and kissed his feet, and anointed them with the ointment. - Luke 7:37-38

Of the three women mentioned in Luke as those who traveled with Jesus, one was "Mary, called Magdalene, from whom seven demons had gone out" (Luke 8:2). How did this woman come to be part of Jesus's entourage? We don't have those details, but it was traditionally believed that Mary had a falling out with her family in Bethany. Perhaps the falling out sent her on a downward spiral that led her to Magdala, a lively port city on the western coast of Israel. Or perhaps Mary moved to Magdala and fell in with the wrong crowd there, for Magdala was known as a town with a high number of pagan citizens. Whatever the reason, Mary lived many miles away from her family and led a life that made her susceptible to evil ways. That is, until the day she encountered our Lord.

Early in Jesus's ministry, just one chapter ahead of Luke's naming of Mary Magdalene as one of the women with Jesus, we meet a penitent woman. "A woman in the city, who was a sinner, having learned that he was eating in the Pharisee's house, brought an alabaster jar of ointment. She stood behind him at his feet, weeping, and began to bathe his feet with her tears and to dry them with her hair. Then she continued kissing his feet and anointing them with the ointment" (Luke 7:37-38).

The Pharisee, a man named Simon, silently admonished Jesus for allowing the sinful woman to touch him. Reading his thoughts, Jesus turned the admonishment around on the Pharisee, telling him a parable in which two men had their debts cancelled. Jesus asked, "which of them will love him more?" The Pharisee replied, the one with the greater debt. Jesus said, "You have judged rightly." Then he chastised the Pharisee for his lack of hospitality saying,

"Do you see this woman? I entered your house; you gave me no water for my feet, but she has bathed my feet with her tears and dried them with her hair. You gave me no kiss,

Figure KK

but from the time I came in she has not stopped kissing my feet. You did not anoint my head with oil, but she has anointed my feet with ointment. Therefore, I tell you, her sins, which were many, have been forgiven; hence she has shown great love. But the one to whom little is forgiven, loves little" (Luke 7:44-47). At this point, Jesus turned to the woman and told her that her sins were forgiven.

> **The one to whom little is forgiven loves little.**
> **Luke 7:47**

Thus, we have the healing of Mary Magdalene. Whether this scene took place before or after Jesus dispelled the seven demons, we do not know. In fact, there is no mention here, or

Figure LL

anywhere in the Gospels, about when and how Jesus expelled the seven demons that tormented Mary.

WE ALL HAVE DEMONS

The twelve were with him, as well as some women who had been cured of evil spirits and infirmities: Mary, called Magdalene, from whom seven demons had gone out, Joanna, the wife of Herod's steward Chuza, Susanna, and many others who provided for them out of their resources. - Luke 8:2-3

What does Luke mean by *seven demons*? This has been interpreted as literally being possessed by demons, as suffering from dissociative personality disorder, as well as suffering from several vices, anything from various addictions to adultery to any number of indecencies. "As Biblical exegesis teaches, the expression 'seven demons' could indicate a serious physical or moral malady that had struck the woman and from which Jesus had freed her."[131] In fact, the Catechism points out that there are Seven Deadly Sins which "engender other sins."[132]

Earlier, we talked about the number seven as a symbol of completion. The fact that Mary was freed of seven demons could have meant that she was completely estranged from her family and from God. She may have turned completely away from God and his teachings or may have been shunned completely from attending religious services. To have been associated with a place, highly unusual for a woman of the time, would have meant that Mary had gained quite a reputation. Whatever demons she had, they robbed her completely of her life and her identity until Jesus completely healed her.

Though it's not something many people like to talk about, it's easy to gain a reputation. One only needs to hang out with the wrong people, get caught doing something that is frowned upon, or fall into the trappings of addiction or hedonistic tendencies. We've all found ourselves, at one time or another, doing something we should not have done. In the time of Christ, however, redeeming oneself was not easily accomplished. Once a person was deemed unworthy, they were shunned and cut off from the temple. Without family, true friends, or a place of worship, bad choices can easily become habits which can become a way of life.

Thankfully, we have a merciful God, and we see that mercy working in Mary Magdalene like no other. Luke's Gospel shows us that Mary's life and the lives of the other women with Jesus "had been changed forever by the merciful love of God that had come to them in their suffering and had set them free."[133] Mary was in a low place, living a life of sin, a life inhabited by demons, yet through the mercy and love of Christ, she grew to become one of the most revered saints of all time, a beautiful example of how God's mercy transforms one's soul and one's life. "God's mercy can make even the driest land become a garden, can restore life to dry bones."[134] If Jesus can recreate a sinner such as Mary

Magdalene, transforming her soul, restoring the very bones within, what can he do with you?

A SOUL SAVED

Then he said to her, "Your sins are forgiven." But those who were at the table with him began to say among themselves, "Who is this who even forgives sins?" And he said to the woman, "Your faith has saved you; go in peace." - Luke 7:48-49

Mary, the penitent woman at the feet of the Lord, has sinned gravely, judging by the scene we witness here. She arrives at the home of a pharisee and bathes Jesus's feet with tears, wiping them with her hair, and anointing them with oil. It's fair to say, no matter what sins she committed, she was tormented by demons and is in dire need of forgiveness. Jesus's mercy changes her life forever.

While this scene took place early in Jesus's ministry at the home of Simon the Pharisee, the scene is very similar to the one in which Martha's sister, Mary, bathed Jesus's feet with burial oil. While some scholars claim that this is the same event, recalled twice in two different places of the Gospel, Catholic theologian Father André Feuillet, a highly regarded theologian of the twentieth century, disagreed. He argued that one anointing took place at the beginning of Jesus's ministry, and the other took place, as we have already said, at the end of his ministry, the night before his triumphant entrance into the city of Jerusalem on Palm

Sunday. Father contended that they were both carried out by the same woman—Mary Magdalene. Father Feuillet taught that, "for anyone who seriously reflects upon the subject, it seems unlikely that two different women would have performed such a unique and downright strange act as the anointing of Christ's feet."[135]

What Feuillet concluded is that these anointings were done by the same woman, yet at the same time, two very different women—one was a sinner, throwing herself at the feet of the Lord and asking for forgiveness, while the other was a saved woman, kneeling before the feet of our Lord to shower him with her love. Mary had been transformed from one woman into another through the love of Christ. She was "renewed by God's mercy…loved by Jesus…enable[ing] the power of his love to transform" her life.[136] "As the great French Dominican preacher Henri Lacordaire put it, there were two anointings carried out by one soul, two different anointings indeed but one heart conceived them both.[137]

When Mary approached Jesus for the first anointing, she was still living in sin and, whether cured of her demons or not, was in need of forgiveness. When Mary approached Jesus for the second anointing, she was a dear friend and companion of Christ. Her sins had been forgiven, and she was once more at her home with her family in Bethany. Theologians point to this passage as a clue to the distinct separation of the anointings: "Now a certain man was ill, Lazarus of Bethany, the village of Mary and her sister Martha. It was Mary who anointed the Lord with ointment and wiped his feet with her hair, whose brother Lazarus was ill" (John 11:1-2).

Remember, as we discussed earlier, the raising of Lazarus took place before Passover, *before* the woman identified as his sister anointed Jesus's feet with the burial oil; yet John is clearly referencing an event that took place earlier in Jesus's ministry in which Mary anointed Jesus's feet with oil and then dried them with her hair (something not done in the second scene). As he has done on other occasions in his Gospel, John is building upon what the other evangelists described. It is in the very next chapter that John gives us a detailed account of Mary's second anointing, as though his mention of the earlier anointing was to remind us that Mary, the repenting sinner, has anointed Jesus's feet before. However, this time, we see Mary the faithful servant anointing Jesus in her family home, truly a new incarnation of spirit. This faithful servant, anointing the feet of the Lord with burial oil, is given instructions that she will need to follow only a week later. When Judas tells Jesus that the oil should be sold for the poor, Jesus answers, "Let her keep it for the day of my burial" (John 12:7). Mary will, indeed, need the oil on Easter morning.

The two women who anointed Jesus were indeed different women, just as we become different women after encountering and spending time with Christ. Nobody is ever the same after a true

> No one shall return by way of the gate by which he entered. (Ezekiel 46:11).

encounter with Christ. We all become different people. One of my favorite images of this is from the book of Ezekiel. In his vision of the new temple (a clear foreshadowing of Christ as the New Temple), the Lord told Ezekiel that "When the people of the land come before the Lord at the appointed feasts, he who enters by the north gate to worship shall go out by the south gate; and he who enters by the south gate shall go out by the north gate: no one shall return by way of the gate by which he entered" (Ezekiel 46:9-11).

Nobody leaves the temple the same way they enter. Nobody who meets Christ is the same. Perhaps with that in mind, we *can* see Mary of Magdala as two different people—the Mary before Christ and the Mary after. She has been transformed from one person into another. No wonder she prefers to sit at the feet of Jesus rather than being anxious about many things.

Think about the first time you encountered Christ, really, truly encountered him. Think about the first time you realized you could have a real, intimate relationship with him. Didn't that change you in some way? Didn't it make you want to know him better, to spend more time with him, to get to know him in a deeper, more meaningful way? Do you long to sit attentively at his feet, soaking up his words and his very presence? Do you want to follow him, to walk the same path to Heaven? Perhaps that is what led you to this moment, to this study—the desire to follow Jesus from your first encounter all the way to Calvary.

THE MARYS, WEEPING TOGETHER

But standing by the cross of Jesus were his mother, and his mother's sister, Mary the wife of Clopas, and Mary Magdalene. - John 19:25

On Good Friday, all but one of the twelve ran away. The men whom Christ chose, the ones who were supposed to be strong and courageous, ran away. It was the women who stayed to witness all that happened to Jesus. "Many women were also there, looking on from a distance; they had followed Jesus from Galilee and had provided for him. Among them were Mary Magdalene" (Matthew 27:55-56). These same women followed Jesus through the streets of Jerusalem to the top of Calvary. Most of the disciples hid, afraid of being caught and suffering the same fate as Jesus, except for John the Beloved Apostle and three women named Mary.*

Of course, Jesus's mother was there. How could she not be? Beside her was her sister, another Mary.* With them was Mary Magdalene. Once again, we find Mary weeping at the feet of the Lord, his mother and spiritual brother at

---

* Matthew also mentions Mary, the Mother of James and John (Matthew 27:55), and Mark tells us that "among the women were Mary Magdalene, and Mary the mother of James the younger and of Joses, and Salome, who, when he was in Galilee, followed him, and ministered to him; and also many other women who came up with him to Jerusalem" (Mark 15:40).

* This was the Virgin Mary's sister-in-law, Joseph's brother's wife.

her side; and when Joseph of Arimathea claimed the body of Jesus, it was Mary Magdalene who comforted Mary, Jesus's mother, at the tomb (Matthew 27:61). Oh, how well she knew the hurt Mary was feeling. After all, she had wept outside the tomb of her brother.

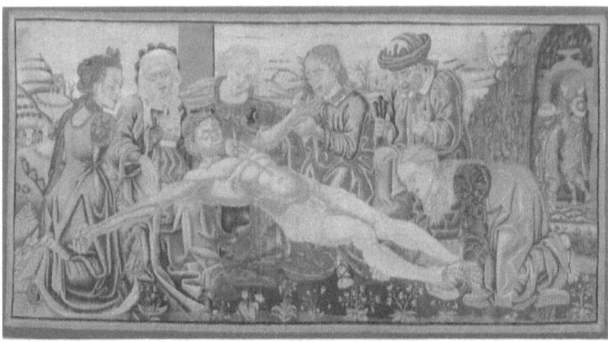

Figure MM

Mary of Magdala learned many things from the example of Jesus's mother; and in his beloved friend, Jesus was able "to see a reflection of his own dear Mother in her soul."[138] Spending so much time with the Blessed Mother would have changed Mary in the same way that spending time with Jesus changed her. Like a mother to the Apostles herself, Mary Magdalene "provided for them out of her means" (Luke 8:3). She became more contemplative, meditating on Jesus's words (Luke 10:38-42). She moved him to tears at the tomb of Lazarus (John 11:35). She showered Jesus with love and spared no expense to show her adoration (John 12:1-8). She was there for him at every pivotal moment, including his passion and death (Matthew 27:55, Mark 15:40, John 19:25).

After the crucifixion, Jesus's disciples were gathered in the Upper Room, hiding, praying, and seeking guidance. They were broken, full of despair, and devoid of hope. I imagine that Mary our mother tried to comfort them, tried to tell them that her son would return, and that Martha tried her best to get them to eat and keep up their strength. I can see Mary of Magdala holding the hands of young John and the others who were seeking comfort. Like any mother or mother figure, the women would have held back their tears and strengthened themselves to tend to the needs of others. Mary would have followed the example of her sister, Martha. She would have taken charge. This is why she was up early on that Sunday morning, heading to the tomb with the spices and oils needed to properly bury her Lord, the very oil she used a week earlier to anoint Jesus's feet at the home of her sister, Martha.

CALLED BY NAME

Jesus said to her, "Woman, why are you weeping? Whom do you seek?" Supposing him to be the gardener, she said to him, "Sir, if you have carried him away, tell me where you have laid him, and I will take him away." Jesus said to her, "Mary." She turned and said to him in Hebrew, "Rabboni!" - John 20:15-16

It is through Mary Magdalene and Mary our Mother, as well as Elizabeth, Esther, Judith, Hannah, Rachel, Rebekah, and the rest, all the way back to Eve, that we can encounter Christ in countless ways and learn to be the person he has called us to be. Like Mary Magdalene, we can and will become changed women if we allow Christ—and his mother—to mold us and shape us into the image of Christ and to model his mother. When we do that, we are given the beautiful pleasure of hearing Christ call us by name.

Mary, "the other Mary" (wife of Joseph's brother, Clopas, mother of James), Salome and/or Joanna went to the tomb (Matthew 28:1, Mark 16:1, Luke 24:10). An angel appeared to them and said, "Do not be afraid; for I know that you seek Jesus who was crucified. He is not here; for he has risen, as he said. Come, see the place where he lay. Then go quickly and tell his disciples that he has risen from the dead, and behold, he is going before you to Galilee; there you will see him" (Matthew 28:5-7) and "Why do you seek the living among the dead? He is not here, but has risen. Remember how he told you, while he was still in Galilee, that the Son of man must be delivered into the hands of sinful men, and be crucified, and on the third day rise" (Luke 24:5). The women returned to the disciples and told them of the news, and Peter and John ran to the tomb. They still did not understand and left in confusion.

Only Mary Magdalene, alone, afraid, and amazed at this discovery, remained at the tomb weeping, unable to fill the last command the Lord gave her—to use her oil to prepare his body for burial. One can't help but wonder what she was thinking as she stood there, the jar of oil in her hand. Surely, she recalled Jesus's admonishment of Judas and his instructions that Mary take care of his body. Was she also thinking about what Jesus had done for her brother? Did that cause her to remember his recent words, "You will weep and mourn, while the world rejoices; you will grieve, but your grief will become joy" (John 16:20)? Did she have the faith of Mother Mary that her weeping

> **"You will weep and mourn, while the world rejoices; you will grieve, but your grief will become joy" (John 16:20).**

would become joy, or is the detail that she went to the tomb "while it was still dark" a clue that she was still blind to what was to come?[139]

As Mary stands by the tomb, the angels ask, "Woman, why are you weeping?" (John 20:13). Once again, we have someone being called, 'Woman.' The angels are elevating the status of Mary from a disciple to an Apostle, redefining who she is and what her purpose is. After Mary explains to the angels that she believes someone has taken the Lord away, she turns and sees a man she thinks is the gardener. She asks if he knows where the Lord has been taken. "Jesus said to her, 'Mary'," and she recognized him

Figure XX

(John 20:16). Mary responded to Jesus, calling him "Rabbi," not recognizing the change in their relationship, the change in her, the redefining of everything—her being, her mission, the world.

The risen Jesus gave Mary a mission, and his instructions have great theological depth. She is to go to the disciples (and the rest of the world) and tell of the Resurrection.[140] Jesus called her by name, then sent her back to the others, proclaiming, "I have seen the Lord" (John 20:18). "Mary has progressed from being 'in the dark,' fixated on the reality of Jesus' death, to the belief that Jesus has been raised. And the risen Jesus has brought her to a higher level of relationship, for his disciples can relate to him no longer only as teacher but also as the Lord himself, who is simultaneously their 'brother'."[141]

That morning, beginning when Mary walked with the other women in the dark to the tomb, she went from being a woman of contemplation to a woman of action. She had learned that both are necessary to follow Jesus.

We all await this moment in our lives, this redefining, this new relationship, the moment when Jesus calls our names. We often look past Jesus, not recognizing him, not seeing his face in the crowd, not knowing his voice when he speaks. We can't see past our own thoughts, fears, worries, assumptions, and prejudices. We expect Jesus to look or sound a certain way, the way we see him, and not always as he is. And then comes that moment when we each hear Jesus speak our name.

I've heard women say, "I listen, but I don't hear him" or "I try to figure out what he wants from me, but I don't understand." Mary expected Jesus to look a certain way, to sound a certain way, and we do the same. We are confronted with Jesus every day of our lives. We look past the homeless because Jesus would not look like them. We ignore those who hunger and thirst for his word because they don't have the same values we do. We turn away from sinners, from modern-day lepers, from tax collectors, and prostitutes because they will make us unclean. We shake our heads when we think a task is too hard and lofty, or too small and unworthy because Jesus doesn't want us to do *that*. That would be asking too much or too little.

There are many ways the Lord calls our name. He may speak to us through family members, friends, colleagues, priests, spiritual advisors, and even strangers. Not everyone has a grand purpose. We can't all be Mother Teresa or the Pope. We don't all have the means to establish holy communities or open hospitals. Many of us can't philosophize like Aquinas, reason like Merton, or write like Augustine. But every single one of us can live our daily lives like Mary Magdalene. Jesus said of Mary, "She has done what she could" (Mark 14:8). This is all we can hope for— that Jesus recognizes that we did all that we could with what we had.

We can all repent of our sinful ways and make a daily effort to walk beside the Lord. Each of us can help others out of our means, whether we are as rich as Solomon or as poor as the widow in Mark's Gospel. We need to recognize that these people are often markers on our journeys, helping us to move to the next place along our paths.

The Widow's Mite

And he sat down opposite the treasury, and watched the multitude putting money into the treasury. Many rich people put in large sums. And a poor widow came, and put in two copper coins, which make a penny. And he called his disciples to him, and said to them, "Truly, I say to you, this poor widow has put in more than all those who are contributing to the treasury. For they all contributed out of their abundance; but she out of her poverty has put in everything she had, her whole

---

We can all read or listen attentively to scripture, to the words of the Lord, and meditate on their meaning in our lives. Everyone can wash the feet of those who need compassion and bathe with perfumed oil those who need to be showered with love and mercy. We can all remain by someone's side in their time of need, pray for them, comfort them, offer to look after their needs—both physical and spiritual. And we can all bring the spices of our lives—sweet and bitter—to meet the needs of others. We can run back to our loved ones and companions and tell them the Good News, that we have seen the Lord!

A MIISSIONARY'S MESSAGE

"Do not hold on to me, because I have not yet ascended to the Father. But go to my brothers and say to them, 'I am ascending to my Father and your Father, to my God and your God.'" Mary Magdalene went and announced to the disciples, "I have seen the Lord"; and she told them that he had said these things to her. - John 20:17-18

Archbishop Fulton Sheen so beautifully said, "Mary was always at his feet. She was there as she anointed him for burial; she was there as she stood at the Cross; now in joy at seeing the Master, she threw herself at his feet to embrace them. . . She was to break the precious alabaster box of His Resurrection so that its perfume might fill the world."[142]

It was Mary, following the order from Christ, who took the news of the Resurrection back to the disciples, and it was Mary who took the Good News to France after Christ's Ascension. Called the Apostle of the Apostles by St. Thomas Aquinas, Mary "had the privilege" of seeing angels, acting as an "intermediary between angels and people;" she had the dignity of looking upon the risen Christ; and she had "the office of an apostle" with the task of announcing the resurrection to the disciples and the world.[143]

Mary's transformation—through forgiveness of sins and through the redefining of whom she is by the angels—and the mission that she was assigned by Christ are the same for all of us. "We are called to seek Jesus intensely and with great love, allowing him to possess our hearts and change our lives…[and] to bear witness to the reality of the risen Jesus and the transforming power of his love available to all who seek it."[144] We all are changed by Jesus's love, and we, through our Baptism, are given the charge of being priests and missionaries to the world.

An oral tradition within the Church tells us that, after the death, resurrection, and ascension of Jesus, a boat left Israel for France. In that boat were Saint Maximin, Mary Jacobe, Salome, Marcelle, Cedonius and Sara, Martha, Lazarus, and their sister, Mary Magdalene. The boat landed on shore, and Mary Magdalene began her missionary work in Provence, teaching the people about Jesus and encouraging frequent consumption of the Eucharist. On the mountain of La Sainte Baume, Mary lived out the remaining years of her life.[145]

Mary never stopped worshipping at the feet of the Lord, never stopped mediating on his words, and never stopped announcing his Good News to the world. This, too, is our call. No matter what we have going on in our lives, no matter how busy or distracted we become, we must always humbly worship the Lord, meditate on sacred scripture and the teachings of the Church, partake in the sacraments, and spread the Good News.

CONCLUSION

THE BLANK COLUMN

Now, Master, you may let your servant go in peace, according to your word, for my eyes have seen your salvation, which you prepared in the sight of all the peoples: a light for revelation to the Gentiles, and glory for your people Israel. - Luke 2:29-32

In the Duc in Altum Church in Magdala, there is a circle of eight columns. Seven of these columns have names on them: Mary Magdalene; Susana and Joanna; Mary and Martha; Salome, mother of James and John; Simon Peter's mother-in-law; Mary, wife of Cleopas; and the unnamed women who followed and supported Jesus. The eighth column is blank and represents you and me and all the women throughout all of time who have followed and still follow Jesus. Standing next to that column, hearing the explanation of the blank column, it is impossible not to shed tears.

Figure 00

We are mothers, grandmothers, wives, sisters, soldiers, teachers, nurses, rulers, sinners, sufferers, worriers, meditators, and weepers. God calls all of us to take part in his mission.

There are ninety-three women mentioned by name in the Bible and many, many more who are nameless. Most of us will remain nameless in the eyes of history and the Church at large, but we will always be known by name to the Lord God who calls to us,

> *Fear not, for I have redeemed you; I have called you by name, you are mine. When you pass through the waters I will be with you; and through the rivers, they shall not overwhelm you; when you walk through fire you shall not be burned, and the flame shall not consume you. For I am the Lord your God, the Holy One of Israel, your Savior.*
> - Isaiah 43:1-3

O, woman, daughter of God, you are being called. Your sins are forgiven, and you have found favor with God even as you do the best that you can. You have a mission, to "go, then, to all peoples everywhere and make them my disciples" (Matthew 28:19).

Let your name be carved on that column. Say to the Lord, "May it be done to me according to your word" (Luke 1:38). Then follow the cairns you encounter on your life's journey. Let them lead you to your Heavenly destination.

ABOUT THE AUTHOR

Amy Schisler wrote articles for magazines and newspapers before writing children's books and adult fiction. As a student of history and graduate of the University of Maryland's School of Library and Information Science, Amy's background in writing and research led her to delve more deeply into the history of her faith.

For over fifteen years, Amy has taught Bible studies at Saints Peter and Paul Parish in Easton, Maryland. She also teaches an online Bible study for women wishing to grow deeper in their faith. In addition, she leads women's retreats and pilgrimages. She had taken pilgrims to the Holy Land, Guadalupe, and Fatima and is has several more pilgrimages in the works.

Amy and Ken, her husband of thirty years, teach marriage preparation classes for the Diocese of Wilmington, Delaware. Amy is the coordinator of altar ministries for the Chapel of St. Michael in St. Michaels, Maryland, where she serves as an Extraordinary Minister of the Eucharist and Lector. In 2017, Bishop Francis Malooly presented Amy with the Order of Merit for the Diocese of Wilmington in recognition of her outstanding contributions to the diocese. In 2022, Amy earned her Certificate of Theology from the Augustine Institute.

Amy writes inspirational fiction rich in her Catholic faith along with children's books, devotionals, and a blog which is read by people around world. The recipient of numerous national literary awards, including the Illumination Award for the best books in Christian literature, LYRA award, Independent Publisher Book Award, International Digital Award, and the Golden Quill Award as well as honors from the Catholic Press Association and the Eric Hoffer Book Award, Amy's writing has been hailed "a verbal masterpiece of art" (author Alexa Jacobs) and "Everything you want in a book" (Amazon reviewer). Amy's books are available internationally, wherever books are sold, in print, ebook, and audiobook formats.

Follow Amy at:
http://amyschislerauthor.com
http://facebook.com/amyschislerauthor
https://instagram.com/AmySchislerAuthor

Scan to go to Amy's Website

ACKNOWLEDGMENTS

This study has been in the works since 2021 when I awoke on Easter Sunday with the certainty that God wanted me to combine my writing skills with the insight I have gained while studying and teaching the Bible for many years. As a student of history and avid learner of theology, I see now that God was leading me in a direction I never knew I would go.

There are so many people I'd like to acknowledge without whom I could not have put this together and would not have been able to create the workbook or video that goes along with this book. First, my husband, Ken; our daughters, Rebecca, Katie Ann, and Morgan; and my parents, Richard and Judy, are my biggest cheerleaders, supporters, marketing team, and critics. You all pushed me to continue when I wasn't sure where or how to go.

The many women in the Bible studies I lead have been so supportive, and I would never have had the courage to step out of my fiction-writing comfort zone to do this without them. I'd like to especially thank Anne Novey, Marian Grammer, Millie Houck, and Julia Miller for critiquing my work. Special thanks also goes to Regina Bell, Gloria Freihage, Millie Houck, Julia Miller, and Naomi Richards for being part of the study which helped put the final touches on the project.

Thank you, Liv Harrison, for reading the first draft and providing me with such a beautiful preface. I am blessed and humbled by your praise. Thank you, David Hyman, tour guide extraordinaire, for allowing me to film throughout our last pilgrimage and for showing and teaching me things I didn't know about the women of the Old Testament. Thank you, Father Nash, Pastor of Saints Peter and Paul Church in Easton, Maryland, for your friendship, your continued support, and for allowing me to use the chapel to film the lecture portion of the video series.

Finally, I must thank Father Michael Angeloni, Associate Pastor of Saints Peter and Paul Church. Your willingness to read my work, and your unwavering support of my career and mission, mean the world to me. You have been a true shepherd, guide, and friend.

ARTWORK

All artwork used in this book is the property of Amy Schisler or in the public domain according to US and other copyright laws.

Figure A (P. 17) - Kunsthistorisches Museum, Austria

Figure B (P. 22) - Eve and Her Two Boys, From My Mother's Bible Stories, 1896

Figure C (P. 25) - Sarah Presenting Hagar to Abraham, Adriaen van der Werff, 1699, SchleiBheim State Gallery, Bavaria

Figure D (P. 28) - Sarah and Abraham Hosting Three Angels, 1914

Figure E (P. 33) - The birth of Jacob and Esau, Cornelis Cort, 1563, British Museum

Figure F (P. 34) - Isaac Feels Jacob as Rebekah Looks On, James, Tissot, 1903

Figure G (P. 37) - Sunday Afternoon on the Island of La Grande Jatte. Georges-Pierre Seurat (1859–1891). Metropolitan Museum of Art.

Figure H (P. 45) - Wandering Heroes, Lillian Louise Price, 1865, Library of Congress

Figure I (P. 48)- Rachel and Leah on either side of Moses, Michelangelo, 1542-1545, San Pietro in Vincoli

Figure J (P. 50) - Dante's Vision of Rachel and Leah, Gabriel Rossetti, Dante, 1855, Walker Art Gallery

Figure K (P. 56) - Pharaoh and the Midwives, James Tissot, 1896, Jewish Museum, New York

Amy Schisler

NOTES

[1] (B. R. Barron, Daily Gospel Reflections)

[2] (John Paul II, Mulieris dignitatem)

[3] (Aquinas, Summa Theologica)

[4] (John Paul II, Letter of Pope John Paul II to Women)

[5] (John Paul II, General Audience)

[6] (Catholic Church) 369

[7] (John Paul II, Familiaris Consortio) 25

[8] (Catholic Church) 375

[9] (Christmyer) 12

[10] (John Paul II, Familiaris Consortio) 19

[11] (PRIDE: Definition of PRIDE by Oxford Dictionary on Lexico.com)

[12] (DePreter)

[13] (DePreter)

[14] (DePreter)

[15] (DePreter)

[16] (R. Barron 82)

[17] (Avtzon)

[18] (Olojede)

[19] (Olojede)

[20] (Avtzon)

[21] (John Paul II, Mulieris dignitatem)

[22] (Vamosh) p. 27

[23] (Great Adventure Bible 65)

[24] (Sered)

[25] (Swann 59)

[26] (Golding)

[27] (McKenna) loc 546

[28] (McKenna) loc 548

[29] (McKenna) loc 560

[30] (Freedman) Mekhilta d'Rabbi Yishmael 16:35:1

[31] (Freedman) Targum Micha 6:4.

[32] (Trible)

[33] (Winship)

[34] (Freedman) *Tanchuma, Tzav 13.*

[35] (The World Holocaust Remembrance Center)

[36] (The World Holocaust Remembrance Center)

[37] (The World Holocaust Remembrance Center)

[38] (McKenna) loc 1377

[39] (Christmyer) p. 323

[40] (S. a. Hahn)

[41] (Vamosh) p. 41

[42] (McKenna) loc 1474

[43] (Christmyer) p. 355

[44] (Mitch)

[45] (Mitch)

[46] (Christmyer) p. 435

[47] (Christmyer) p. 435

[48] (McKenna) loc 1573

[49] (Andreasen) p. 180

[50] (Andreasen) 188

[51] (Andreasen) 198

[52] (Catholic Church) 2737

[53] (Vanhoozer) 98

[54] (Christmyer) p. 664

[55] (Francis, The strength in our weakness)

[56] (Catholic Church) 494

[57] (Christmyer) p. 1565

[58] (Catholic Church) 488

[59] (S. Hahn) p. 40

[60] (S. Hahn) p. 41

[61] (S. Hahn) p. 42

[62] (Catholic Church) 489

[63] (S. Hahn) p. 126

[64] (Sheen, The Wrold's First Love: Mary, the Mother of God) 29

[65] (Catholic Church) 964

[66] (Francis, Sunday Angelus of 14 February 2015)

[67] (John Paul II, General Audience)

[68] (Christmyer) p. 1565

[69] (Francis, Homily Of His Holiness Pope Francis On The Solemnity Of Mary, Mother Of God XLVIIII World Day Of Peace)

[70] (Augustine)

[71] (John Paul II, Redemptoris Mater) 14

[72] (R. Barron) p. 94

[73] (S. Hahn) p. 100

[74] (R. Barron) p. 96

[75] (Pius XII)

[76] Hahn, p. 65

[77] (B. R. Barron, Daily Gospel Reflections)

[78] (Sheen, The Wrold's First Love: Mary, the Mother of God) 26

[79] (Martin SJ) loc 2870

[80] (Clement of Alexandria and Wilson)

[81] (Vamosh) p. 7

[82] (Vamosh) p. 9

[83] (Vamosh) p. 9

[84] (Sefaria Community)

[85] (John Paul II, Familiaris Consortio) 13

[86] (John Paul II, Familiaris Consortio) 25

[87] (Paul VI)

[88] (John Paul II, Familiaris Consortio) 22

[89] (John Paul II, Familiaris Consortio) 22

[90] (John Paul II, Familiaris Consortio) 23

[91] (John Paul II, Familiaris Consortio) 14

[92] (John Paul II, Familiaris Consortio) 49

[93] (B. R. Barron, Daily Gospel Reflections) Bar21

[94] (McKenna) loc 1672

[95] (McKenna) loc 1761

[96] (McKenna) loc 1698

[97] (D'Ambrosio) 157

[98] (Chrysostom) loc. 21002

[99] (Catholic Church) 2610

[100] (Falbo) 41

[101] (Falbo) 55

[102] (Catholic Church) 2616

[103] (D'Ambrosio) 85

[104] (Cavins) 14:45 minutes

[105] (D'Ambrosio) 117

[106] (Catholic Church) 164

[107] (D'Ambrosio) 117

[108] (McKenna) loc 1774

[109] (McKenna) 825

[110] (McKenna) 957

[111] (Christmyer) p. 1539

[112] (R. Barron) p. 18

[113] (Francis, Sunday Angelus of 23 March 2014)

[114] (Davidson) 85

[115] (Gray) 247

[116] (Gray) 256

[117] (Martin) 80

[118] (Chrystosdom) loc 312

[119] (Francis, Sunday Angelus of 21 July 2019)

[120] (Francis, Sunday Angelus of 21 July 2019)

[121] (Davidson) 86

[122] (Francis, Sunday Angelus of 21 July 2019)

[123] (Davidson) 96

[124] (Christmyer) 1641

[125] (Martin SJ) loc 5153

[126] (Martin) 218

[127] (Francis, Sunday Angelus of 21 July 2019)

[128] (Francis, Sunday Angelus of 21 July 2019)

[129] (Davidson) 20

[130] (Davidson) 22

[131] (St. Mary Madgalene, Disciple of the Lord)

[132] (Catholic Church) 1866.

[133] (D'Ambrosio) 131

[134] (Francis, Urbi et Orbi, Easter Message)

[135] (Davidson) 27

[136] (Francis, Urbi et Orbi, Easter Message)

[137] (Davidson) 32

[138] (Davidson) 78

[139] (Martin) 331

[140] (Martin) 337

[141] (Martin) 338

[142] (Sheen, Life of Christ) 594

[143] (Aquinas, Commentary on the Gospel of John)

[144] (Martin) 339

[145] (Davidson) 13-14

BIBLIOGRAPHY

Andreasen, Niels-Erik A. "The Role of the Queen mother in Israelite Society." *The Catholic Biblical Quarterly* 45.2 (1983): 179-194.

Aquinas, Thomas. *Commentary on the Gospel of John.* 2519.

—. "Summa Theologica." *Volume 29, The Old Law 1a2ae. 98-105.* n.d.

Augustine, Saint. *The Works of Saint Augustine, A Translation for the 21st Century, Sermons III On the New Testament.* Vol. III. Brooklyn: New City Press, 1991. sermon.

Avtzon, Levi. "Who Was Deborah the Nurse? And Why Did Jacob Mourn Her Death?" 2018. *Chabad.* 3 May 2021. <https://www.chabad.org/library/article_cdo/aid /4199139/jewish/Who-Was-Deborah-the-Nurse.htm#footnote2a4199139>.

Barron, Bishop Robert. "Daily Gospel Reflections." *Memorial Of The Blessed Virgin Mary, Mother Of The Church.* Des Plaines, IL: Word on Fire Catholic Ministries, 24 May 2021.

—. "Daily Gospel Reflections." *Memorial of St. John Vianney.* Des Plaines, IL: Word on Fire Catholic Ministries, 4 August 2021.

Barron, Robert. *Catholicism.* New York: Image Books, 2011.

Catholic Church. *Catechism of the Catholic Church.* Vatican City: Libreria Editrice Vaticana, 2012.

Cavins, Jeff. "Bible in a Year." *Messianic Checkpoint: The Gospel of Mark*. By Father Mike Schmitz. 2021. Podcast.

Christmyer, Sarah. "Editor." *Living the Word Catholic Women's Bible*. Notre Dame: Ave Maria Press, 2022.

Chrystomdom, St. John. *Homilies on the Gospel of John*. Houston, TX: Veritatis Splendor Publications, 2012.

Clement of Alexandria, St. and translated by William Wilson. "The Stromata, or Miscellanies." *Ante-Nicene Fathers Vol. 2*. Buffalo: Christian Literature Publishing Co., 1985.

D'Ambrosio, Marcellino. *Jesus, The Way, The Truth, and the Life*. West Chester, PA: Ascension Press, 2020.

Davidson, Father Sean. *Saint Mary Magdalene, Prophetess of Eucharistic Love*. San Francisco: Ignatius Press, 2017.

DePreter, Olivia. "Women of Genesis: Mothers of Power." *Denison Journal of Religion: Vol 10, Article 5* (2011).

Falbo, Giovanni. *St. Monica, the Power of a Mother's Love*. Boston: Pauline Books and Media, 1993.

Francis, Pope. "Homily Of His Holiness Pope Francis On The Solemnity Of Mary, Mother Of God XLVIIII World Day Of Peace." Vatican City: The Holy See, 1 January 2015. Speech.

—. "Sunday Angelus of 14 February 2015." Vatican City, 14 February 2015.

—. *Sunday Angelus of 21 July 2019*. Vatican City: Vaticnan City Press, 2019.

—. "Sunday Angelus of 23 March 2014." Vatican City, 23 March 2014.

—. "The strength in our weakness." *Morning Meditation In The Chapel Of The Domus Sanctae Marthae*. Vatican City: The Holy See, 18 June 2015. Homily.

—. "Urbi et Orbi, Easter Message." Vatican City: The Holy See, 31 March 2013. Speech.

Freedman, H, Maurice Somon, and Judah J. Slotki. *Midrash Rabbah*. London: Soncino Press, 1939.

Golding, Nechama. *Rachel's Tomb (Kever Rachel)*. 2017. 21 April 2021.

Gray, Tim and Cavins, Jeff. *Walking With God: A Journey Through the Bible*. Des Plaines, IL: Ascension Press, 2010.

Great Adventure Bible. West Chester, PA: Ascension Press, 2018.

Hahn, Scott and Kimberly. *Genesis to Jesus, Journey Through Scripture*. New York: Costella Publishing Company, 2011.

Hahn, Scott. *Hail, Holy Queen*. New York: Image Books, 2001.

John Paul II, Pope. "Familiaris Consortio." *Apostolic Exhortation On The Role Of The Christian Family In The Modern World*. The Holy See: The Holy See, 22 November 1981.

—. "General Audience." *Mary's co-operation is totally unique*. Vatican City: The Vatican Library, 9 April 1997.

—. "Letter of Pope John Paul II to Women." *Letter of Pope John Paul II to Women*. Ottawa: Canadian Conference of Catholic Bishops, 1995.

—. "Mulieris dignitatem." *Apostolic letter on the Dignity and Vocation of Women*. The Holy See: The Holy See, 15 August 1988.

—. "Redemptoris Mater." Vatican City: The Holy See, March 25 1987.

Martin SJ, John. *Jesus: A Pilgrimage; Kindle Version*. New York: HarperCollins, 2014.

Martin, Francis and Wright, William. *The Gospel of John*. Grand Rapids, MI: Baker Academic, 2015.

McKenna, Megan. *Not Counting Women and Children: Neglected Stories from the Bible. Kindle Edition.* New York: Orbis Books, 1994.

Mitch, Scott Hahn and Curtis. *The First and Second Book of Samuel*. San Francisco: Ignatus Press, 2016.

Olojede, F. "The "First Deborah" – Genesis 35:8 in the literary and theological context." *Acta Theologica* (2016): 133-151.

Paul VI, Pope. *Gaudium et Spes*. Vatican City: The Vatican, 1965.

Pius XII, Pope. "Allocution to the faithful assembled at St. Peter's AAS 46." Rome: The Holy See, 1 November 1954. Papal Audience.

PRIDE: Definition of PRIDE by Oxford Dictionary on Lexico.com. n.d. 21 April 2021.

Sefaria Community. *Midrash: Bereshit Rabbah*. 2021. Sefaria Community. July 2021. <https://www.sefaria.org>.

Sered, Susan. "Rachel's Tomb and the Milk Grotto of Mary: Two Women's Shrines in Bethlehem."

Journal of Feminist Studies in Religion, Vole 2 (1986): 7-22.

Sheen, Fulton J. *Life of Christ*. New York: Doubleday, 1977.

—. *The Wrold's First Love: Mary, the Mother of God*. San Francisco: Ignatius Press, 1952.

"St. Mary Madgalene, Disciple of the Lord." *Vatican News* 22 July 2016: https://www.vaticannews.va/en/saints/07/22/st--mary-magdalene--disciple-of-the-lord-.html.

Swann, Ingo. *The Great Apparitions of Mary*. New York: Crossroad Publishing Company, 1996.

The World Holocaust Remembrance Center . *Women of Valor*. 2021.

Trible, Phyllis. "Miriam: Bible." 20 March 2009. *Jewish Women: A Comprehensive Historical Encyclopedia.* 20 April 2021.

Vamosh, Miriamm Feinberg. "Women at the Time of the Bible." Vamosh, Miriamm Feinberg. *Women at the Time of the Bible* . Herlzia, Israel: Palphot Ltd, 2007.

Vanhoozer, Kevin J. *Dictionary for Theological Interpretation of the Bible*. Grand Rapids: Baker Academic, 2005.

Winship, David G. "The Need to Sing." 8 January 2019. *Sefaria.* 27 April 2021. <https://www.sefaria.org/sheets/152436.7?lang=bi&with=About&lang2=en>.